AUSTRALIAN
EXPLORERS

Unlocking the Great South Land

AUSTRALIAN
EXPLORERS

Unlocking the Great South Land

R OBERT C OUPE

NEW
HOLLAND

First published in Australia in 1998 by
New Holland Publishers (Australia) Pty Ltd
Sydney • Auckland • London • Cape Town

14 Aquatic Drive Frenchs Forest NSW 2086 Australia
218 Lake Road Northcote Auckland New Zealand
86 Edgware Road London W2 2EA United Kingdom
80 McKenzie Street Cape Town 8001 South Africa

National Library of Australia Cataloguing-in-Publication Data:

Coupe, Robert.
Australian explorers: unlocking the great south land

Includes index.
ISBN(13) 978-1-86436-285-5
ISBN(10) 1 86436 285 5.

1. Australia – Discovery and exploration – Juvenile literature.
2. Australia – History – 20th Century. I. Title.

994

Publishing General Manager: Jane Hazell
Publisher: Averill Chase
Designer: Patricia McCallum
Cartography: DiZign Pty Ltd
Reproduction: Dot'n'Line
Printer: Kyodo Printing Co. (S'Pore) Pte Ltd

10 9 8 7 6 5

Picture Credits
All pictures (including cover) were obtained from the National Library of Australia,
except the following:
- Coo-ee Historical Picture Library: pp 9, 60 (bottom)
- State Library of New South Wales: p 11 (top)
- West Australian Newspapers Ltd: p 58.

CONTENTS

INTRODUCTION

On 18 January 1788, a fleet of 11 vessels with billowing sails entered Botany Bay on the east coast of New South Wales, as the eastern part of Australia was then known. The voyage from England had lasted just over eight months. This event was the beginning of modern Australia. Now known as the 'First Fleet', these ships carried almost 1500 people. About half of them were crewmen, soldiers and officials. The other half were convicts — men and women who had been convicted of crimes in England and were sent to New South Wales as a punishment. In charge of the First Fleet was Captain Arthur Phillip, a 49-year-old lieutenant in Britain's Royal Navy. His job was to found a settlement which would become a colony of Britain. Botany Bay was chosen because, 18 years earlier, an expedition led by Captain James Cook had sailed along the east coast of New South Wales and had landed at Botany Bay. On his return to England, Cook had recommended it as an ideal place for a settlement.

Phillip, however, was not so impressed. He found the bay too shallow and unprotected. So he decided to explore further afield. A little to the north of Botany Bay, Cook had passed an inlet with what looked like a large harbour. He named it Port Jackson but did not sail in to investigate. Phillip took three boats and sailed north into Port Jackson, which he thought was the 'best harbour in the world', and on whose shores he decided to establish his settlement. By discovering Port Jackson, which is now better known as Sydney Harbour, Arthur Phillip became the first of many adventurers who journeyed in and around the continent of Australia to discover just what kind of country it was.

The people on the First Fleet knew very little about the land they were coming to; as did the British authorities who had sent them. Cook had sailed up the east coast and in the 200 years or so before that, other ships from Europe, mainly Holland, had explored other parts of the Australian coast. But no one from Britain or Europe had the slightest idea of what lay further inland. Cook and others had seen and had contact with groups of dark-skinned people who lived around the edges of the continent.

An early depiction of an Australian Aborigine.

Ships of the First Fleet in Sydney Cove.

These caravels were the types of ships in which Portuguese merchants and explorers sailed in the 1500s.

around the Cape of Good Hope, he sailed due east across the Indian Ocean, taking advantage of the strong westerly winds known as the 'Roaring Forties'. As he approached the west coast of Australia, which of course he did not know was there, Brouwer turned north to sail to Java. In those days, ships' navigational instruments were often unreliable, and it was not long before some ships travelled too far to the east and either landed, or were wrecked, on the west coast of Australia.

Discoveries in the west

Dirk Hartog was probably the first Dutch sea captain to land on the west coast. In October 1616, his ship, the *Eendracht*, was sailing to Java by the new route when it was blown too far east. Hartog and his crew landed on a small island near Shark Bay, which is now called Dirk Hartog Island. We know about this landing because Hartog recorded his visit by nailing a pewter plate to a tree. On this plate he inscribed a message which recorded his visit. The point where the plate was left is now known as Inscription Point. Hartog named this land Eendrachtland after his ship, but he reported it to be dry and worthless.

Throughout the rest of the 1600s many other Dutch ships arrived at different parts of the continent's west coast, but the Dutch were not interested in settling the country. It was not until 1688 that the first Englishmen landed in Australia.

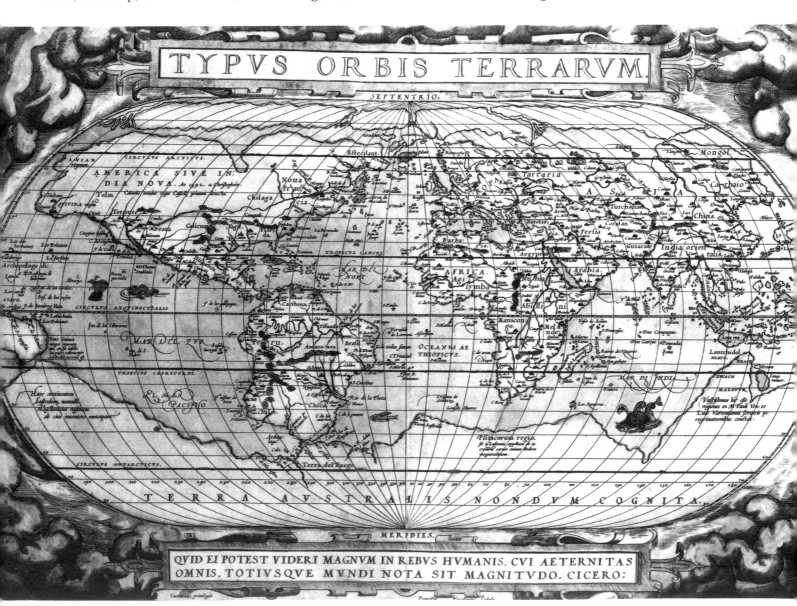

This map of the world was published in Holland in 1570. It includes the imaginary 'unknown south land'.

In that year the *Cygnet*, a pirate ship that had been sailing around the area to the north of Australia attacking and robbing other ships, came ashore on Australia's north-west coast for attention to her repairs. On board was the adventurer William Dampier. When he arrived back in England, Dampier wrote an account of his travels, titled *A New Voyage Round the World*, which he published in 1697. In his account Dampier depicted Australia, which by that time was generally known as New Holland, as a dry, sandy, waterless land inhabited by what he described as the 'miserablest people in the world'.

In spite of Dampier's poor opinion, the English government was interested in this new, unknown land, and decided to send Dampier back to find out more about it. In 1699 Dampier was given command of an old and leaky ship, the *Roebuck*, and was told to return and explore the coasts of New Holland and New Guinea. The voyage was a disaster. Dampier sailed up much of the west coast, from Shark Bay to Roebuck Bay, both of which he named, then sailed north to explore the north-west coast of New Guinea. But the *Roebuck* sank before it got home and Dampier arrived back in England in disgrace as a passenger on another ship.

William Dampier

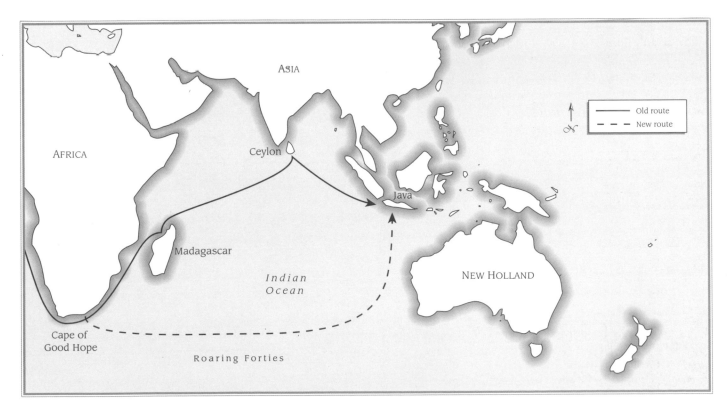

How Dutch ships reached the Dutch East Indies.

ABEL TASMAN

The island of Tasmania is named after Abel Tasman, the Dutch sailor who, in 1642, became the first European to set foot on its shores. Tasman was driven ashore on the island's south-east corner by a storm at sea. He named it Van Diemen's Land after Anthony Van Diemen, the then governor-general of the Dutch East Indies. It was Van Diemen who had sent Tasman on a voyage to discover as much as possible about the still largely unknown 'south land'.

Van Diemen was an ambitious Dutch official who wished to expand the Dutch empire in the region. Tasman was also ambitious. In 1633, at the age of 30, he had left Holland as an ordinary seaman bound for Batavia. Only a year later he was given command of a Dutch trading vessel. He returned to Holland in 1637 but set out again for the Dutch East Indies the following year. In 1639 he was second-in-command of a voyage of exploration in the north Pacific, and after that took part in journeys to various parts of east Asia. So in 1642, when Van Diemen chose him to lead a major voyage, Tasman was already an able and experienced explorer. Van Diemen hoped that Tasman might discover 'rich mines of precious metals and fertile regions' in the great continent to the south. He instructed Tasman to make contact with any inhabitants he encountered and to attempt to communicate with them and then establish a trading relationship.

A land of giants

In August 1642, Tasman set out from Batavia in charge of two ships, the *Heemskerck* and the *Zeehaen*. It was a well-organised expedition and Tasman was prepared for a voyage that would last as long as a year. The ships first sailed south-west to the island of Mauritius, then further south until the Roaring Forties drove them east to the south of the Australian continent. If they had continued in this direction they would have travelled well past the southern tip of Tasmania. However, wild weather drove them further north and, at the end of November 1642, Tasman made his historic landing at a spot which he named, appropriately, Storm Bay. Tasman did not stay there long and did not meet any of the inhabitants. Some of his crew, however, claimed to have heard human voices, which may have meant that the Aborigines were observing the newcomers from hiding

Abel Tasman

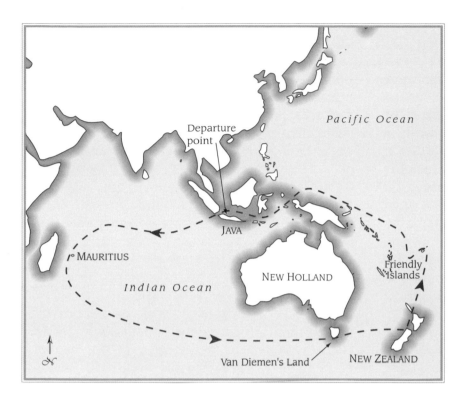

Tasman's 1642 voyage.

Exploring the north

In January 1644, less than a year after his return, Van Diemen sent Tasman on another voyage, this time to discover whether New Guinea was joined to Australia. Tasman did not succeed in solving this mystery because big seas and strong winds forced him south into the Gulf of Carpentaria. However, he surveyed most of the coast of northern and north-west Australia before sailing north back to Batavia. This second important journey proved that the north and the western parts of New Holland were part of the one great landmass. Tasman's explorations had added considerably to Europeans' understanding of the unknown south land — its shape was gradually becoming clearer.

Anthony Van Diemen died in the following year, so too did the Dutch interest in exploring the southern continent. Tasman later undertook several more voyages before he died in 1659, but none of these were around the Australian coast.

places nearby. The visitors noticed that footholds had been cut into some of the trees and these were so far apart that they imagined the land to be inhabited by a race of giants.

At this stage, on 5 December 1642, Tasman made a fateful decision: to continue sailing eastwards. If, instead, he had sailed northwards, he would probably have discovered that Tasmania was not part of the Australian continent and then may have been able to explore the southern and eastern coasts of the continent. Eight days after leaving Tasmania, Tasman's ships came to the west coast of New Zealand and their crews became the very first Europeans ever to see that country. He then turned north, visited the islands of Tonga and Fiji, and then sailed westwards over the north of New Guinea on his way back to Java. As well as discovering new territories, Tasman's important voyage showed that the landmass of Australia did not extend all the way to the south pole.

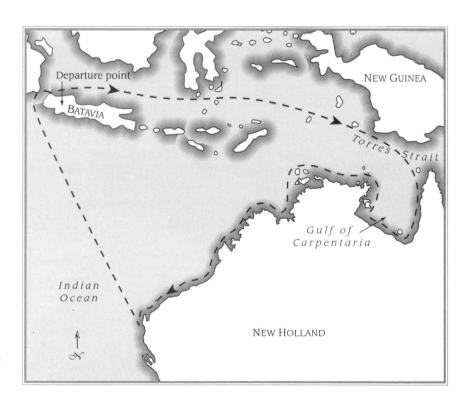

Tasman's 1644 voyage.

JAMES COOK

James Cook was one of the greatest maritime explorers of all time, and one who changed the course of Australian history. Like Abel Tasman, he came from a humble background. He was born in 1728 of poor parents in the small village of Marton in Yorkshire, in the north of England. Cook's father was a farm labourer and as a boy Cook also did farm work, but he was fortunate enough to gain some basic education at the village school. He began his seafaring life at the age of 18, at first on a collier and then as a sailor on trading ships. When he was 26 he joined the Royal Navy and soon made a favourable impression on his superiors with his surveying and navigation skills.

On 27 October 1757, his 29th birthday, Cook was made commander of a warship, HMS *Pembroke*, and was sent to Canada to survey the Saint Lawrence River near the city of Quebec, which at that time was a French possession. Cook's survey of these dangerous, rocky waters enabled the British fleet to sail safely through and capture Quebec from the French. In 1763 he was sent back to Canada to survey and chart the coasts of Newfoundland, which he did with great skill and accuracy. In 1766 Cook observed and recorded details of an eclipse of the sun and sent a report of the event to the Royal Society of

London, an organisation devoted to scientific research. Before he was 40 years old, then, Cook had established a reputation as a sea captain, surveyor, map-maker and navigator, and as an observer and accurate recorder of natural events.

Secret instructions

Every 105 years the planet Venus crosses between the sun and the earth. Members of the Royal Society knew that this event, known as the transit of Venus, was due to occur on 3 June 1769, and they were anxious to send a team of observers to the South Pacific to record it. The British navy was also keen on this venture — an accurate observation of the transit of Venus would help scientists gain a better idea of the distance between the earth and the sun, and this would allow sailors to draw up more accurate navigational charts.

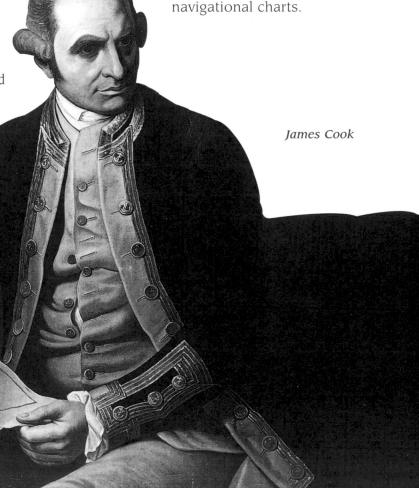

James Cook

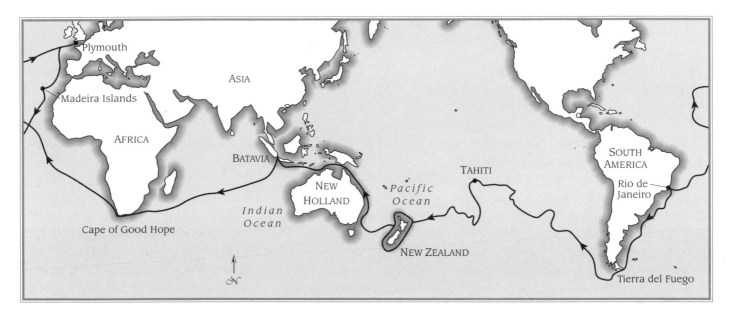

The voyage of the Endeavour.

Cook was chosen to lead this expedition and was given command of a three-masted former collier, the *Endeavour*, with orders to sail to Tahiti. Among the 94 men aboard the *Endeavour* were a number of scientists, including the botanists Joseph Banks and Daniel Solander, and the astronomer Charles Green. What nobody on board knew was that Cook had secret instructions from the British government to continue sailing west from Tahiti in an attempt to solve the remaining mysteries of the unknown south land, and to claim that land for Britain. When the *Endeavour* sailed from Plymouth on 26 August 1768, even Cook did not yet know what these instructions were. They were in a sealed envelope which was to be opened only when the job of observing the transit of Venus had been completed.

Dangers at sea

In those days sailing was a dangerous occupation. Not only was there the risk of accidents on board, or of being wrecked in violent seas or on rocky coasts, there were also diseases that afflicted people at sea. One of the worst of these was scurvy. This terrible disease resulted from a lack of fresh food, particularly foods containing vitamin C, and from living for long periods in unhygienic conditions. Sea captains expected up to one in three of their crew to die of scurvy during a long voyage. Although Cook did not understand the importance of vitamin C, his long years at sea, as

both an ordinary sailor and an officer, had taught him that fresh food and hygiene could help to prevent scurvy. As soon as the *Endeavour* put to sea, Cook insisted on strict hygiene. Every man had to bathe in cold water at least once a day, bedding was aired on deck and the ship was regularly fumigated and scrubbed down. On the way to Tahiti, the *Endeavour* made three stops — at the Madeira Islands off the coast of Africa, at Rio de Janeiro in Brazil, and at Tierra del Fuego near the southern tip of South America — and at each place Cook took on board as much fresh food as possible. When fresh food ran out, the men were forced to eat pickled cabbage. Those who refused to eat it were flogged. When the *Endeavour* returned to England after a voyage that had lasted three years, not one man had died of scurvy, although 38 had died of accidents and other diseases, such as dysentery and malaria.

In the Pacific

On rounding the tip of South America, Cook sailed north-west across the Pacific, directly to Tahiti, where he arrived eight weeks later — a considerable feat of navigation at that time. Cook's party spent three months on Tahiti. During this time they built a wooden stockade which they named Fort Venus, successfully observed and recorded the transit of Venus, and established friendly relations with the native Tahitians. On 13 July 1769, the *Endeavour* sailed out of Mataval Bay followed by a flotilla of canoes. The quest for the great southern continent had now begun.

Cook sailed south from Tahiti, hoping to come upon land. But after weeks of fruitless searching, he ran into bad weather and changed direction, heading west towards New Zealand. Cook knew of New Zealand's existence from the maps Tasman had drawn a century and a quarter earlier. He spent the next six months sailing around both islands of New Zealand and drawing accurate maps. In this way he proved once and for all that this was not part of the sought-after south land. At this point Cook could have turned around for home, but he decided to travel further west. He knew that a land known as New Holland must lie in that direction. Europeans had visited and explored parts of its west and north coasts, but its east coast and the size of the land still remained a mystery.

A banksia bloom, named after Sir Joseph Banks.

Exploring a new coast

At the end of March 1770, the *Endeavour* left New Zealand. Almost three weeks later, early on the morning of 19 April, Lieutenant Zachary Hicks, who was the officer on watch, became the first European that we know of to have seen the east coast of Australia. He woke Cook, who decided to change direction and head northward rather than into the strong winds that were buffeting the ship from the west.

Cook realised that he was some distance north of where Tasman had landed and he wondered whether Van Diemen's Land was part of the same landmass. It would be almost another 30 years before this question was finally answered.

Point Hicks, near the south-eastern tip of the Australian mainland, was just the first of many places that Cook named as, over the next four months, the *Endeavour* made its way northwards along the eastern coast of the Australian mainland. The first landing was made in an inlet just south of Sydney, which Cook named Botany Bay. Here the party came ashore for a week. Two Aborigines armed with spears tried to prevent the landing, but were driven off by gunfire. Botany Bay made a favourable impression on Cook and his men: the soil seemed good enough for cultivating crops and there were plenty of birds and animals to hunt for food. While they were ashore Joseph Banks and his assistants gathered many plant specimens to take back to England.

A narrow escape

On the night of 11 June, the *Endeavour*'s voyage almost came to a tragic end. As the ship sailed through the dark and dangerous waters of the Great Barrier Reef, it struck a coral reef and water rushed in. The crew managed to keep the ship afloat by pumping and covering the hole with sailcloth. When the ship eventually floated free, a large piece of coral remained stuck in the hull. This acted like a plug and kept the ship afloat until it could put ashore near the mouth of a river, now known as the Endeavour River, near the present-day town of Cooktown. The ship took two months to repair and during this time Cook took the opportunity to explore the surrounding area. He reported favourably on the land and described the local Aborigines as an 'inoffensive race'.

An artist's impression of Cook's landing at Botany Bay.

Early in August, the *Endeavour* continued its northward journey. On 22 August, Cook landed on an island near the tip of Cape York where he raised the British flag. He declared the eastern part of Australia to be a British possession and named it New South Wales. Cook had now achieved both missions on which he had been sent.

The *Endeavour* then sailed to Batavia on the island of Java, where it was repaired properly before it sailed back to England. It arrived home on 13 July 1771. On the return journey a total of 32 men died from diseases. Only six had been lost on the journey to Australia.

The Endeavour *aground after striking a coral reef.*

Cook and his party on Possession Island in Torres Strait.

BASS AND FLINDERS

George Bass and Matthew Flinders were the last of the great maritime explorers of the Australian coastline. In a number of voyages, both together and separately, they provided answers to the most important questions that still remained about the shape of the Australian continent and the island of Tasmania.

Bass and Flinders became friends in 1794. They met on board the *Reliance*, which set sail from England bound for Port Jackson. Flinders, aged 20, was the master's mate and already an experienced sailor — he had previously been on one expedition to the Pacific and had taken part in a naval battle against the French. Bass, aged 23, was the ship's doctor. The two young men soon found they had a lot in common: both came from the same part of England — Lincolnshire — and Flinders was the son of a doctor. But, most important of all, they both had a great interest in navigation and maritime exploration.

Captain Matthew Flinders

George Bass

The *Reliance* arrived in Sydney in September 1795, and Bass and Flinders immediately made preparations to explore. Bass had brought with him from England a rowing boat less than three metres long. He had named it *Tom Thumb* after the tiny fairytale character. The two friends rigged this up with a sail and, just a few weeks after arriving in the colony, sailed south to Botany Bay and explored the Georges River. They arrived back nine days later and the report they made to Governor Hunter led to the establishment of a settlement on the Georges River, which was named Bankstown. The following March they once again sailed south, this time in a larger, but still very small, boat supplied by the governor. It too was christened *Tom Thumb*. This voyage was very nearly their last because, just two days after setting out, the boat was driven violently ashore, south of Botany Bay, by a huge wave. Refloating the boat, they continued south as far as Shellharbour, just south of where Wollongong now stands. On the return journey they discovered and named Port Hacking.

Tasmania is an island!

Later that year, the *Reliance*, with Bass and Flinders on board, sailed to Cape Town to pick up supplies for the colony. The ship returned in June 1797, and in December Bass and six sailors once again sailed south, this time in a nine-metre whaleboat. In a voyage that lasted almost three months, they travelled almost 2000 kilometres. They actually went around the south-eastern tip of the continent and as far west as Western Port. They had almost sailed through the strait now known as Bass Strait, but their supplies were running out and they had to turn around and head for home. Bass was certain that Van Diemen's Land, as Tasmania was then known, was separated from the mainland — the tides he encountered convinced him of that — but he had not yet proved it conclusively.

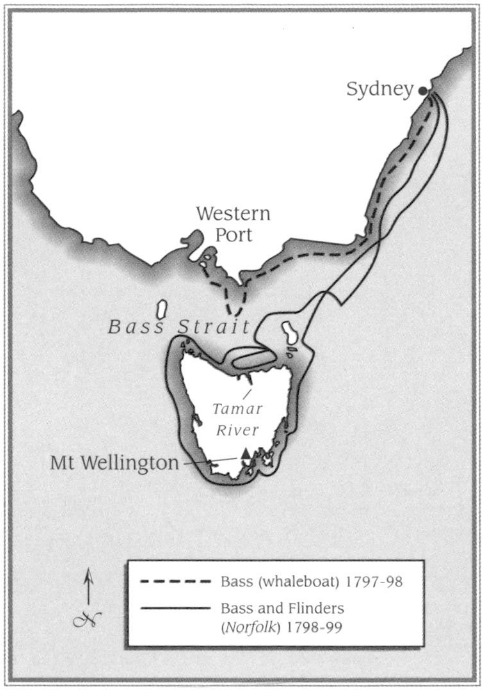

The first circumnavigation of Tasmania.

Proof came early in 1799. In October 1798, a leaky 25-tonne ship, the *Norfolk*, sailed out of Port Jackson with Flinders in command and Bass next in authority. Eight other sailors were on board. In the next three months the *Norfolk* sailed along the northern coast of Van Diemen's Land, southwards along its west coast, then north again up the east coast before returning to Sydney. On the north coast of the island, Bass and Flinders rowed up the Tamar River almost to where Launceston now stands, and on Christmas Day they climbed to the top of Mount Wellington which now overlooks Hobart, the capital of Tasmania. During this voyage, Bass was able to indulge another of his great interests by making detailed studies of birds and the other native animals he encountered.

The elusive body of water that Cook suspected was there, that Bass had gone looking for in his whaleboat and that Bass and Flinders finally sailed right through, was named Bass Strait by Governor Hunter.

Soon after that historic voyage of discovery, George Bass resigned from the Royal Navy to sail trading vessels. In February 1803, he left Sydney on a voyage to Chile in South America. But after his ship, the *Venus*, sailed out of Sydney Harbour, neither it, its crew or its captain was ever seen or heard from again. George Bass' disappearance is one of the enduring mysteries of Australian exploration.

Circumnavigating Australia

In June 1803, perhaps about the same time that George Bass' ship sank somewhere in the Pacific, another ship captained by Matthew Flinders, the *Investigator*, limped into Sydney Harbour. It was the end of an epic voyage that had lasted just under two years. During this time the *Investigator* had completed the first-ever voyage right around the Australian continent.

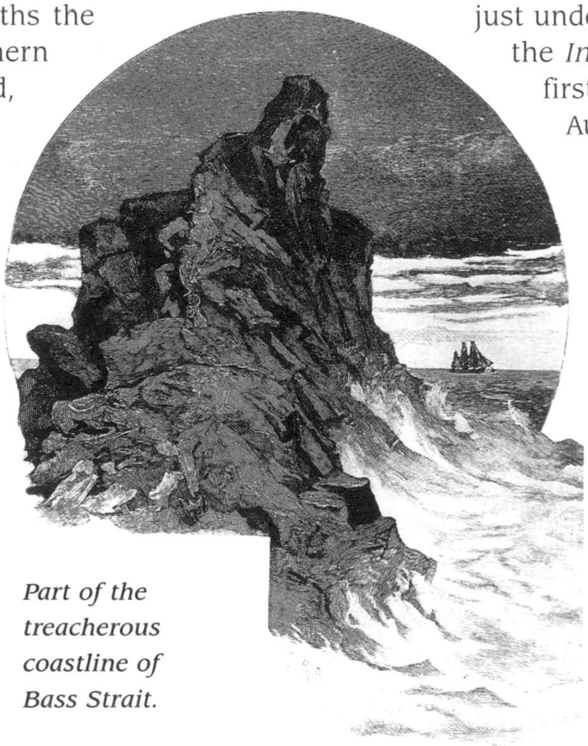

Part of the treacherous coastline of Bass Strait.

Early in 1800 Flinders had returned to England, where he wrote and had published a detailed account of his and Bass' explorations. He dedicated this to Sir Joseph Banks, the famous botanist who had sailed with Cook. Banks used his influence to have Flinders promoted and put in charge of an expedition to sail around the Australian coastline to chart those parts of it that were still unknown. Although Bass and Flinders

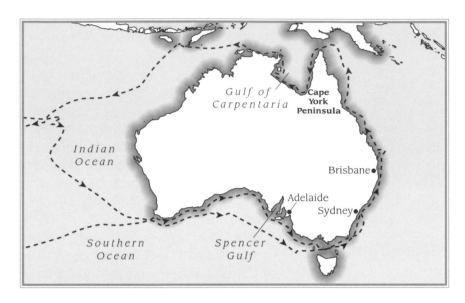

Flinder's 1801–03 voyage on the Investigator.

had sailed through Bass Strait and around Tasmania, no European sailors had yet observed most of the southern coast of the continent.

The *Investigator* set sail in July 1801. Six months later it reached the south-western tip of the Australian continent. It sailed close to shore through what is now called the Great Australian Bight, and Flinders accurately surveyed and charted the coastline. As he sailed past the towering cliffs that form much of Australia's southern coastline, Flinders imagined that a vast inland sea must lurk behind them. This theory, which Flinders was the first to state, later dominated Australian land exploration. During the 19th century expedition after expedition set out to find this inland sea that people were convinced must exist.

Sailing on, Flinders investigated Spencer Gulf, which he thought could lead to a great river that flowed from deep within the continent, and Gulf St Vincent, near the eastern shore where Adelaide now stands. The *Investigator* then landed on a large island just south of these gulfs. Here the crew found huge numbers of kangaroos, which provided a welcome source of fresh meat. This island, the largest one around the Australian coast, is today called Kangaroo Island.

Early in May 1802, the *Investigator* reached Sydney and remained there for more than two months to undergo repairs. Even before it left England the ship was in very poor condition; many of the timbers beneath the copper sheathing that covered its hull were already rotting away. By the

time it had rounded Cape York and sailed around the coasts of the Gulf of Carpentaria, it was leaking so badly that Flinders considered returning to Sydney. Having come so far, however, he decided to continue and headed for the island of Timor to take on supplies. Most of the three–month voyage back to Sydney took the *Investigator* well clear of the coast. It sailed south-west into the Indian Ocean, then eastwards across the Southern Ocean through Bass Strait and up the eastern coast. During this last part of the voyage seven members of the crew died from dysentery or scurvy. By the time it arrived in Sydney almost everyone on board was ill and weak. The *Investigator* itself had barely been able to complete the journey and was in no state to sail back to England.

A prisoner of the French

Despite his magnificent achievement against very heavy odds, Flinders was not satisfied. He wanted to return to Australia with a better ship to complete his exploration. But bad luck and another leaky ship foiled him again. Just one month after reaching Sydney, Flinders sailed for England as a passenger aboard the *Porpoise*, but this ship came to grief on a coral reef in the Pacific. Flinders took command of the ship's lifeboat and managed to navigate his way back to Sydney. He was given command of a small schooner, the *Cumberland*, and set sail again. But as it crossed the Indian Ocean, the *Cumberland*, like the *Investigator* before it, started leaking badly and Flinders was forced to put in at the island of Mauritius, which was a French possession. France was then at war with England and the French governor of the island arrested Flinders as a spy and imprisoned him for a period of six years.

Flinders eventually arrived back in England in 1810. Although he was still only 36, his health was broken and he was not fit for further exploration. He lived for another four years. During this time he published an account of his journeys under the title *A Voyage to Terra Australis*. In this book he repeatedly referred to the continent as 'Australia', the name by which it later came to be known.

BLAXLAND, LAWSON AND WENTWORTH

The Great Dividing Range is a string of hills and mountains that runs from north to south along almost the entire length of the eastern side of the continent. This range is never far from the eastern coast and in many places is clearly visible from the sea. The section immediately west of Sydney is known as the Blue Mountains. This is because of the blue haze that seems to settle on them when viewed from a distance, a result of the evaporated oil from eucalypt leaves.

Even though these mountains rise a mere 1000 metres above sea level, this region is one of spectacular beauty with deep gorges, sheer golden brown sandstone gorges and plunging waterfalls.

It is now one of Australia's scenic wonders and a region that attracts hundreds of thousands of tourists and holiday-makers every year.

But for the early settlers in Sydney the Blue Mountains were a source of mystery and frustration. As the convict numbers increased during the 1790s and the population of the colony was further swelled by the arrival of free settlers, more land was needed to grow crops and graze the large flocks of sheep that had been brought to the colony. But the Blue Mountains stood like a great wall, a natural barrier that blocked the westward expansion of the colony and frustrated people's natural desire to know what lay beyond.

This 1820s painting of Wentworth Falls shows the cliffs that foiled early attempts to cross the Blue Mountains.

As you travel west from Sydney along the road that now leads up and over the Blue Mountains, you arrive, at an altitude of about 300 metres, at the township of Blaxland. About 24 kilometres further on, at an altitude of about 700 metres, you pass through the township of Lawson. Another six kilometres further on you reach the village of Wentworth Falls, which is almost 900 metres above sea level. These three places are named after Gregory Blaxland, William Lawson and William Charles Wentworth. In 1813 they became the first European people we know of to find a route across the Blue Mountains. They may not have been the very first, as it is possible that one or more escaped convicts got there first. But if they did, they probably would not have advertised their achievement! What we can be certain of is that the expedition of Blaxland, Lawson and Wentworth was the one that showed the way across the mountains and opened up a route to the west.

Gregory Blaxland

Early attempts

During the 25 years before 1813, expedition after expedition had ventured into these mountains. The first official expedition, in 1789, managed to travel only 24 kilometres in three days before being stopped by towering cliffs. In 1796 George Bass tried his luck but had to return after 15 days. In 1802 Governor King sent out a party under the leadership of George Barrallier. He hacked his way through the valleys and gorges, penetrating deeper into the area than any previous expedition, until he too came upon towering walls of sandstone. These were the huge cliffs that are now know as the Kanangra Walls.

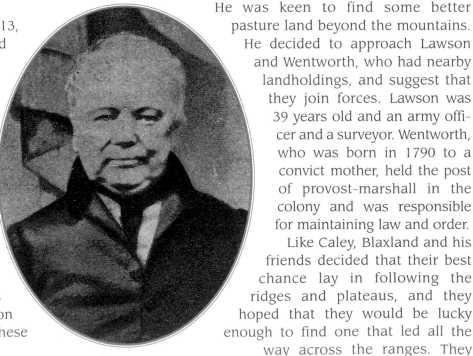

William Lawson

The problem with all these attempts was that the explorers decided to follow the rivers which seemed to flow from the mountains. They knew that English and European rivers flowed from high up in hills and mountains down to the plains below. But these rivers flowed through deep gorges, and even at their source the explorers found themselves not at the mountain peaks, but still in deep valleys hemmed in by cliffs. In 1804 an expedition led by George Caley tried a new way. Setting out from Richmond, north-west of Sydney, Caley decided not to follow the valleys, but the ridges that rose above them. Ten days after setting out Caley found himself blocked, not by cliffs that rose above him, but by a ridge which brought him to the edge of a plunging precipice.

Blaxland's idea

The idea for the 1813 expedition came from Gregory Blaxland himself. Blaxland was a wealthy 35-year-old settler who grazed cattle on his farm near Saint Marys, west of Sydney. He was keen to find some better pasture land beyond the mountains. He decided to approach Lawson and Wentworth, who had nearby landholdings, and suggest that they join forces. Lawson was 39 years old and an army officer and a surveyor. Wentworth, who was born in 1790 to a convict mother, held the post of provost-marshall in the colony and was responsible for maintaining law and order. Like Caley, Blaxland and his friends decided that their best chance lay in following the ridges and plateaus, and they hoped that they would be lucky enough to find one that led all the way across the ranges. They set out from Blaxland's farm on 11 May 1813, with four convict servants, four horses and five dogs. For a few days it seemed that they too would be stopped by high cliffs, but eventually they found the one ridge that led continuously between the valleys and gorges. The way forward was difficult and dangerous. They had to cut through thick, scrubby bush and often travelled along narrow rocky ledges where a false step or a slip would send them hurtling to their death. Many times they had to retrace their steps and find new ways forward. Although they travelled up to 15 kilometres a day, their progress was less than one-third of that. Eventually, on 28 May, they reached the edge of a mountain which is now known as Mount York and is a few kilometres west of the township of Mount Victoria. From here they looked down on a valley that was 'clear of trees' and 'covered with good grass'. It was, according to

William Charles Wentworth

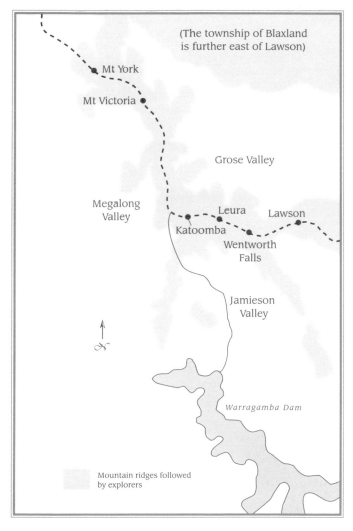

Blaxland, Lawson and Wentworth followed a ridge between the deep valleys of the Blue Mountains.

Blaxland, land which would feed the sheep and cattle of the colony for the 'next 30 years'.

Before returning home Blaxland, Lawson and Wentworth spent three days hacking out a steep track down into this valley. By this time the men were exhausted, sick and almost out of food. They retraced their steps and arrived back on 6 June.

Building a road

Based on information from this pioneering journey, George Evans, the assistant surveyor for New South Wales, was able, later in the same year, to plan the route for a road over the Blue Mountains. Just over a year later, in January 1815, a rough track that was dangerously steep and narrow in some places, had been completed. The building was supervised by William Cox and the work carried out by 20 convicts who were guarded by eight soldiers. It led to where the present-day town of Bathurst now stands and opened the way for settlers and their stock to move into western New South Wales.

EVANS AND OXLEY

It was actually George Evans who led the first expedition right across the Great Dividing Range. In November 1813, Evans set out on the orders of Governor Lachlan Macquarie to plan a road across the mountains. It took him only a week to reach the point beyond Mount York where Blaxland, Lawson and Wentworth had ended their westward journey. Pushing further westward, Evans discovered that still more mountains lay ahead. It would be another four days before he had made his way through the remaining steep and difficult mountain country, and another nine days after that before he reached the point on the western plains where the town of Bathurst now stands. Two days before this, on 7 December, he had come upon a large river which he named the Macquarie River. For the next 10 days Evans and his party followed this river north-west until they

George Evans

turned to retrace their steps. Evans was delighted at the green and fertile plains he had discovered.

Almost 18 months later, in April 1815, a large party jolted its way along the road that Evans had surveyed to the banks of the Macquarie River. Among the travellers were Evans, Governor Macquarie and his wife, William Cox and a man called John Oxley. On 7 May the governor made a speech in honour of Evans and Cox and named the spot as the site of a town to be called Bathurst. Just a week later, Evans set out from Bathurst on a second expedition. This time he travelled south-west in the hope, as he wrote in his journal, that he would find another 'river of some consequence'. He came upon such a stream and followed it westwards for about 80 kilometres. In a further tribute to Governor Macquarie, he named it the Lachlan River.

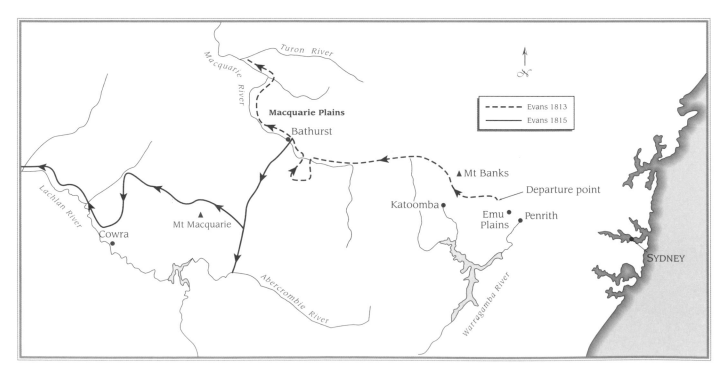

Evans led the first expedition across the Great Dividing Range.

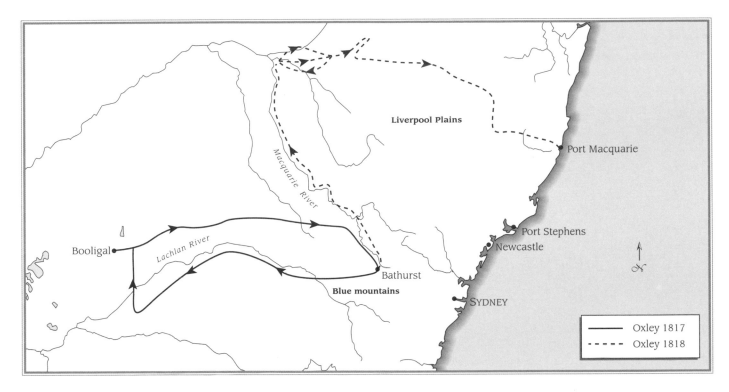

Oxley was accompanied by Evans on both these expeditions.

Legend:
— Oxley 1817
- - - Oxley 1818

Looking for an inland sea

In 1817 Macquarie appointed John Oxley as leader of the next important expedition to the west of the Great Dividing Range. Evans was appointed second-in-command. Oxley was about 34 years old at this time. At the age of about 16 Oxley had joined the British Navy and had arrived in Sydney in 1802. Although he had spent most of his adult life as a sailor and naval officer, in 1812 he was appointed surveyor-general of New South Wales. Oxley's instructions were to follow the Lachlan River, which Evans had discovered two years earlier, and find out where it flowed. Matthew Flinders had suggested that the interior of Australia might consist of a vast inland sea. Perhaps the Lachlan flowed into this sea.

With a team of packhorses that carried portable boats, Oxley and his party departed from Bathurst on 20 April and reached the Lachlan

John Oxley

five days later. They followed the river, some in boats and others along the river bank, only to find that it seemed to peter out in a series of swamps and marshes. Disappointed, Oxley decided to change direction. He first went south-west through country that he described as 'uninhabitable and useless', then north-west. To their great surprise the party came upon a river. Oxley correctly assumed that this was another part of the Lachlan, which they had left five weeks earlier. They followed this part of the river downstream for another two weeks until it too ended in marshy swamps in the middle of what Oxley thought was flat and featureless country. Oxley came to the dismal conclusion that 'the interior of this vast country is a marsh and uninhabitable'. The unhappy party made its way back to Bathurst and arrived there at the end of August. The trek had covered just under 2000 kilometres.

Port Macquarie in the 1820s, soon after John Oxley's expedition arrived there.

Following the Macquarie

Just over a year after setting out on his first expedition, Oxley, with Evans as his deputy, was again sent out by Macquarie. This time they were to follow the Macquarie River which would, perhaps, lead them to a vast inland sea. They left Bathurst on 18 May 1818, but by early July found themselves stranded among reeds. Oxley still thought that they were on the edge of an inland sea, but they had to retreat because the flooding waters of the Macquarie made further exploration unsafe.

Oxley's party then headed east towards the coast and they soon came upon another river, which they named the Castlereagh. In late August, they saw from an elevated vantage point an area of 'the most varied and exhilarating kind . . . plains of the richest description lay before us'. They named them the Liverpool Plains and today they are a rich agricultural and pastoral area. Oxley's party proceeded further east and south-east. They crossed the Great Dividing Range from the west, becoming the first Europeans to do so. In early October 1818, they followed a river, which they named the Hastings, to its mouth at a place they named Port Macquarie, again in honour of the governor. Port Macquarie is now an important town and holiday resort on the New South Wales mid-north coast.

The Warrumbungle Range, seen by Oxley in 1818.

HUME AND HOVELL

In October 1824, an expedition led by 27-year-old Australian-born Hamilton Hume and 38-year-old Englishman William Hovell set out from Appin, about 45 kilometres south-west of Sydney. It was bound for Western Port, the port in Bass Strait that George Bass discovered early in 1798. The object of the expedition was to find out what kind of country lay to the south of the Murrumbidgee River. As well as the leaders, there were four convict men, three horses and five bullocks. There were two carts to carry the food and other equipment, which included a tent, two tarpaulins, guns and blankets. Some of this equipment had been supplied by the governor, Sir Thomas Brisbane, but most of the costs were shared equally between Hume and Hovell. This was the first Australian expedition to use bullocks and it was also the first to take along a baby's pram. Hovell had attached a device to the pram's wheel which, like a modern car's odometer, was designed to measure the distances travelled.

William Hovell

Hamilton Hume

Hovell had been a sea captain and considered himself a good navigator. Hume was already an experienced explorer — he had explored as far south as the plains around Yass — and was also an expert bushman who understood some Aboriginal languages. The two men had met only recently and were an odd pair. Their quarrels and disagreements during the journey almost caused the expedition to be abandoned.

The first major challenge came when they reached the banks of the Murrumbidgee River. They crossed the river by fixing a tarpaulin around the bottom of one of the carts and using it as a boat to ferry across the food and equipment. In later years, Hume and Hovell each claimed the credit for devising this ingenious plan and argued about many other details of the journey. In these arguments the convicts usually supported Hume's accounts, but this may have been because he was friendlier to them than was the rather aloof Hovell.

Into unknown territory

Beyond the Murrumbidgee River, Hume and Hovell were in unknown territory. The countryside was very rugged and mountainous and the way was made more difficult by the hot weather and the swarms of flies that constantly tormented them. In some places they had to retrace their steps to find a way through to the south-west. On 8 November, they caught sight of the snow-covered peaks of the Australian Alps and eight days later, they came upon what Hovell described as 'a very fine river — at least 200 feet [60m] wide, apparently deep' surrounded by level land covered by 'fine alluvial soil'. They had discovered Australia's greatest river and they named it Humes River. A few years later, when Charles Sturt explored the full extent of this river, it would be renamed the Murray. Because of the high banks they were unable to cross at this point, so they travelled westward and made the crossing at a spot near the present Hume Weir. They crossed in a boat they made out of saplings

wrapped in tarpaulin. Once again, both leaders later claimed credit for devising this craft.

As they penetrated further into what is now the state of Victoria, Hume and Hovell crossed and named several major rivers, including the Ovens and the Goulburn. Near the Goulburn they found grassy country that was largely clear of trees and that, according to Hovell, would be ideal land for grazing sheep.

Just south of the Goulburn the party ran into difficulties. They encountered mountains covered with thick bush that scratched their faces and tore their clothes. These seemingly impenetrable mountains were the very southern part of the Great Dividing Range. They hacked their way up a mountain, which they named Mount Disappointment, climbed down again and travelled further west, where they succeeded in finding a way through. As they approached the coast they marvelled at the rich pasture lands through which they passed. In the middle of December they arrived at a bay which,

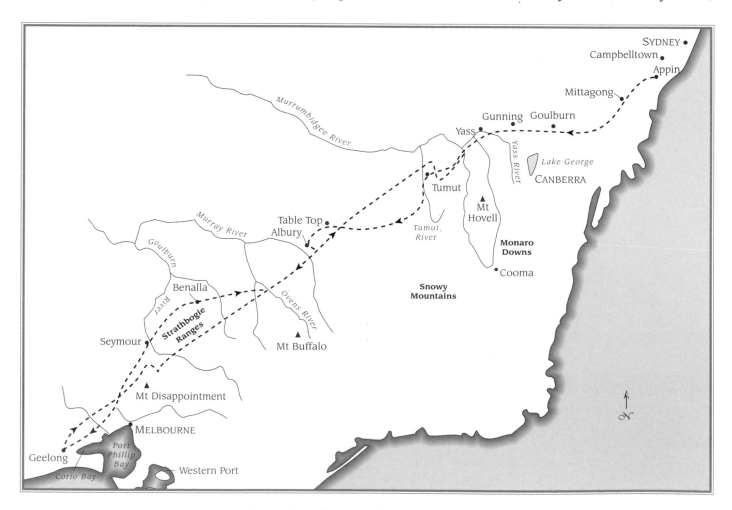

The 1824–25 journey of Hume and Hovell.

Hume and Hovell's expedition crossing the Murrumbidgee in a cart covered by tarpaulin.

according to Hovell's calculations, was Western Port. But his calculations were wrong; his pram for measuring distances had fallen apart during the journey and he had had to rely entirely on compass readings. Where they really were was a place now known as Corio Bay, on the western side of Port Phillip Bay. Western Port was more than 100 kilometres further east.

A costly error

Almost immediately Hume and Hovell began the long and difficult journey home. Several times they ran out of food and survived only by catching fish and shooting kangaroos. They arrived back a

month later and immediately advised the governor of the wonderful grazing land at Western Port. As a result of their report, a group of people set out in 1826 to establish a settlement at Western Port. When they got there they found that instead of the lush grazing country they had been promised, the land was barren and sandy. It was a disappointing sequel to a heroic expedition that had added greatly to the settlers' knowledge of the country. Had Hovell got his calculations right, the area around Port Phillip would probably have been settled ten years earlier than it was, and the history of Victoria and the city of Melbourne may have taken a very different course.

ALLAN CUNNINGHAM

Now famous mainly as the explorer who in the 1820s led the way to some of eastern Australia's richest agricultural and pastoral areas, Allan Cunningham was first and foremost a botanist. He and his brother Richard made detailed studies of the plants and trees of many parts of Australia and New Zealand. Several Australian trees, for example the Tasmanian native myrtle beech (*Nothofagus cunninghamii*), are named after them. Allan Cunningham died in Sydney in 1839 at the age of 47 and 62 years later, in 1901, his remains were dug up and placed within a memorial obelisk in Sydney's Royal Botanic Gardens.

Early explorations

Cunningham arrived in Australia at the end of 1816. Soon afterwards, he was appointed as one of two botanists on John Oxley's expedition to the Lachlan River. For the next five years he was employed as a botanist in detailed surveys of many parts of both the mainland and Tasmanian coasts. In 1822 he suggested to the governor, Sir Thomas Brisbane, that he lead an expedition to find a way through the mountains to the rich and fertile Liverpool Plains, which had been discovered by Oxley in August 1818.

Brisbane agreed, but the expedition was a dismal failure. Cunningham had travelled barely 100 kilometres from Bathurst before he lost his horses and was forced to trek back. He tried again the next year, setting out from Bathurst with five men and five horses. Three weeks later the party was looking down on the Liverpool Plains from a peak which Cunningham named Oxley's Peak, but there seemed to be no way through to them. Cunningham spent several days exploring the area but to no avail; steep cliffs barred his way in every

Allan Cunningham

direction. Admitting defeat, Cunningham moved to the east and discovered many rivers along the way. He then swung westward again, intending to return to Bathurst through the lower parts of the mountains. On 5 June, near the present town of Coolah, he caught sight of part of the lush green plains through a gap in the ranges. Joyfully, he named this gap Pandora's Pass. It was only a matter of months before cattle and sheep were being driven through this pass to the rich region that is now known as New England.

Riches to the north

Cunningham was now keen to push further north to discover what lay there. In 1827, Sir Ralph Darling, who became governor of New South Wales in 1825, supplied Cunningham with six convicts, 11 horses and equipment for a long expedition. The party left from the Hunter Valley on 30 April and 11 days later was in territory that only Aborigines had ever seen. For another three and a half weeks they pushed northward through what Cunningham later described as a 'variety of country'. The area explored included stretches of 'gloomy woods', where they encountered neither 'Indian nor kangaroo', as well as areas of 'barren, brushy tract'.

On 26 May, near the present border between New South Wales and Queensland, they were surprised to find, 'in so arid a region . . . a handsome piece of water . . . evidently very deep' which was 'winding its way to the westward' and which 'received the name of Dumaresq's River'. Ten days later, from a point above this river, Cunningham looked out across a great stretch of open grassy country that later became known as the Darling Downs. This would later become perhaps the richest agricultural area in eastern Australia.

Cunningham's memorial in Sydney's Royal Botanic Gardens.

Cunningham knew that he was now not far from the settlement at Moreton Bay (now Brisbane) where a penal colony had been established in 1824. Cunningham noticed a gap in the mountains and thought it would be possible to pass through it to the coast. But his men and horses were in a weakened state and he decided not to investigate, heading for home instead. This great journey of discovery, covering almost 1300 kilometres in just under three months, arrived back at its starting point in the Hunter Valley on 28 July.

Finding the gap

In July 1828, Cunningham sailed to Moreton Bay to join an expedition that was trying to find a way inland to the Darling Downs. The expedition was led by Captain Patrick Logan who was commander of the settlement at Moreton Bay. When they failed to find a way through, Logan returned to Moreton Bay and left Cunningham with three men to continue the search. Late in August, Cunningham discovered a pass near the one he had seen from the other side of the range more than a year earlier. This pass is now known as Cunningham's Gap.

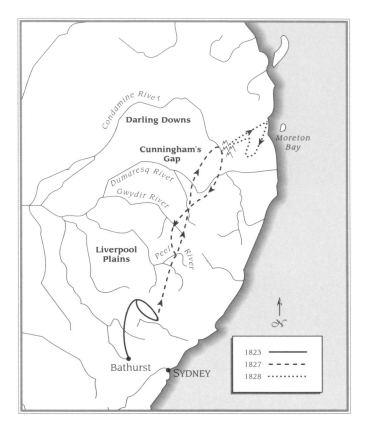

Cunningham's exploration routes.

A cattle station on Queensland's Darling Downs.

CHARLES STURT

Although Hume and Hovell were the first Europeans to find the Murray River, it is Charles Sturt whose name is most closely associated with it. Sturt is often referred to as 'Sturt of the Murray' because of his epic exploratory journey along most of its length. He might just as correctly be called 'Sturt of the desert' because he was the first great explorer to travel deep into the arid interior of the continent and discover its true character.

When Sturt arrived in Sydney in 1827, at the age of 32, he was a captain in the British army and was ambitious to make a name for himself. He had already had an active military career; he had fought against the French in Spain, the Americans in Canada and had also served in Ireland. He was sent to New South Wales on board the *Mariner* and was in charge of the convicts on board. He soon became friendly with some of the most influential people in the colony, including the governor, Sir Ralph Darling, who appointed Sturt as his military secretary, and the explorer John Oxley.

Charles Sturt

In Oxley's footsteps — and beyond

Ever since Matthew Flinders had first suggested it in the 1790s, the theory that there was a large inland sea in the centre of the continent fascinated people. Oxley still believed that the western rivers such as the Lachlan flowed into such a sea, and Darling wanted to put this belief to the test. To the surprise of many, and the anger of some others, Darling appointed Sturt to lead an expedition to follow the Macquarie River further than where Oxley had been able to go in 1817. According to Darling, Sturt had the scientific knowledge necessary for the job, even though he had no experience of land exploration. To make up for this, Governor

Darling appointed the very experienced Hamilton Hume as the second-in-command of the expedition.

The party of 11 men set out from Wellington at the end of 1828, equipped with a boat as well as nautical navigation equipment. Like Oxley more than ten years earlier, they were unable to get beyond the marshes on the Macquarie River. But rather than turn back, Sturt pushed further west and north-west into the dry interior. The country was even drier than usual because it was in the grip of a long drought. They had to depend on Hume's experience to find water in order to survive.

On 2 February 1829, at a spot north-east of the present town of Bourke, the party suddenly came upon what Sturt described as 'a noble stream'. But their excitement turned to dismay when they discovered that the water was salty and unfit to drink. They followed the river, which Sturt named the Darling, for about 100 kilometres before turning in their tracks and heading back to Wellington, where they arrived in late April. Although they had neither proved nor disproved the existence of an inland sea, Sturt now believed that the Darling flowed into such a sea.

Down the Murrumbidgee

Later in 1829 Darling sent Sturt on another river journey, this time to follow the Murrumbidgee as far as possible. The party left Sydney early in November and arrived on the banks of the swiftly flowing Murrumbidgee three weeks later. They followed the banks of the Murrumbidgee past the furthest settled land. Sturt was struck by the beauty of the country that he first passed through, but as he went further west it became progressively sandier and more arid. On 26 December, he decided to abandon the horses and bullock carts in which they had been travelling and proceed further down the river by boat. A whaleboat that they had brought with them in pieces was put together and a smaller boat was built from a tree on the river bank. Eleven days later, Sturt and seven men set out in the whaleboat, towing their supplies behind them in the smaller boat.

Eight days later, at about 3 p.m. on 14 January 1829, the boats and their occupants were swept at great speed into a 'broad and noble river'. Sturt thought this river was probably a continuation of one of the streams that Hume had crossed on his journey with Hovell more than four years earlier. It was in fact the stream they had named the Hume, but which Sturt now renamed the Murray.

During its progress along the rivers, Sturt's party had frequent and friendly contact with groups of Aborigines. But on the morning of 23 January, a warlike group on one of the river's sandbanks seemed ready to hurl their spears at the passing boat. Alarmed, Sturt took aim with his rifle but another group of Aborigines arrived and its leader struggled across to the sandbank and forced the angry group back to the shore. Soon after this unsettling incident the boat came to another stream on the right. Sturt thought, correctly, that it must be the Darling. Still observed from the bank by the warlike Aborigines, Sturt hoisted the Union Jack in the boat and got his men to give three cheers.

Almost four weeks later Sturt's boat drifted into Lake Alexandrina, through which the Murray empties into the sea. It was not the inland sea that Sturt had been looking for, but his journey had answered the major questions about where the great inland rivers flowed.

By this time the men were weak and sick. The return journey was extremely difficult, as they were

Warlike Aborigines confront Sturt's expedition along the Murray on 23 January 1829.

In August 1845, Sturt crossed 'an immense gloomy plain', now known as Sturt's Stony Desert. This painting, which shows Sturt looking out over this desert, gives little idea of the hardships he endured.

forced to row against the current, and it was another two months before, on 11 April, they reached the spot from where they had set out by boat. They camped here and Sturt sent two of the party ahead on foot to find help. The two men arrived back a week later bringing extra supplies with them. A tragic end to an epic expedition had been narrowly avoided.

A boat in the desert

The next 14 years were largely frustrating ones for Sturt. His friend and supporter Governor Darling had left the colony in 1832 and Sturt did not really receive the recognition he felt he deserved. On top of this, his health was not good and his eyesight was failing. But Sturt remained convinced that an inland sea existed and in 1844 he was given approval to undertake an expedition from Adelaide into the interior.

He left Adelaide in August 1844, now an ailing 49-year-old, at the head of a large expedition of 15 men. There were also horses, bullocks, sheep for meat and a boat to launch on the inland sea. It was a frustrating and agonising journey which lasted almost 18 months. The journey took Sturt over vast distances through some of the harshest and driest parts of the continent into what is now the south-west corner of Queensland. At the end of it, in January 1846, Sturt was desperately ill with scurvy and had to be carried back to Adelaide.

His second-in-command, James Poole, had died of scurvy less than a year after they had set out. Sturt's last and most difficult journey finally laid to rest the idea that there was a vast inland sea, but left perhaps the greatest of Australian explorers a sick and disappointed man.

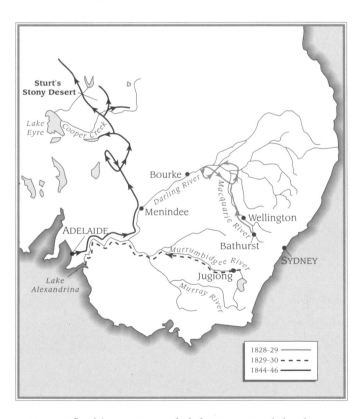

Sturt's final journey revealed there was no inland sea.

THOMAS MITCHELL

Thomas Mitchell was a brilliant man who distinguished himself as a soldier, a naturalist, a draughtsman and surveyor, a writer of scholarly works on a wide range of subjects, and as an explorer. But he was blunt and quick-tempered and was often hard to get along with. When he was sent as assistant surveyor-general to New South Wales in 1827 at the age of 35, he was a major in the army and had an impressive military record.

At the end of 1827, Governor Darling decided to send an expedition to investigate the western rivers and Mitchell assumed he would be the first choice to lead it. When Charles Sturt was chosen Mitchell could not contain his anger and contemptuously referred to Sturt as an 'amateur traveller'. Had Mitchell been on better terms with Darling he may well have got the job. The strong dislike between Sturt and Mitchell continued over the years. In fact, a good deal of the exploring that Mitchell did during the 1830s was motivated by a desire to prove his rival wrong!

Major Thomas Mitchell

Mitchell's first expedition, however, was undertaken in order to prove someone right. In 1831, an escaped convict, George Clarke, was captured in north-western New South Wales and brought back to Sydney. Clarke told stories of a great river which flowed to the sea at the north of Australia. With a party of 17 men and a team of packhorses, Mitchell travelled north-west until he encountered the Barwon River. He followed this, thinking it may be the great northern-flowing stream, only to find that it flowed into another river. Mitchell realised that this river was the one that Sturt had discovered — the Darling.

Investigating the Darling

In April 1835, Mitchell left a station near Orange to head an expedition that he was confident would prove the Darling flowed northward and not, as Sturt believed, into the Murray. A member of this expedition was the botanist Richard Cunningham, the brother of the explorer Allan Cunningham. Less than two weeks after the party left, Cunningham became separated from the party and was killed by a group of Aborigines.

When Mitchell reached the banks of the Darling, he built a stockade to serve as a base camp. He called the stockade Fort Bourke after the governor. However, when he then tried to sail down the river, the water was too shallow for the boats. The stockade had to be abandoned and the expedition continued down the river bank. Just over six weeks later, it reached a point on the Darling near where Menindee now stands. Here the party clashed with a group of Aborigines and at least two Aborigines were shot. As there was no sign that the Darling was about to change direction and flow north, Mitchell decided to return home. It was still not known for certain where the Darling ended up.

In March 1836, Governor Bourke sent Mitchell out again, this time with 27 armed men in case of trouble from Aborigines. His instructions were to continue to follow the Darling to its end. But Mitchell was not keen to prove Sturt correct and, instead of going to the Darling, he went to the Lachlan. He claimed that the severe drought made it impossible for his party to travel into the far west. Mitchell followed the Lachlan until it joined

An Aboriginal corroboree on the banks of the Murray River.

the Murrumbidgee and on 23 May, he came to where it joined the Murray. The next day Mitchell was alarmed by a large group of Aborigines whom

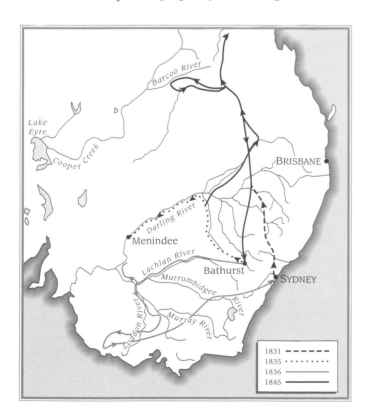

The expeditions of Thomas Mitchell.

he recognised as the same group he had clashed with the previous year. Four days later he decided to set an ambush for the Aborigines. He sent some men into the scrub to 'take them in the flank' while the rest of the party remained behind a hill. A number of Aborigines were shot in the attack and Mitchell gave 'this little hill which witnessed this overthrow of our enemies . . . the name of Mount Dispersion'.

Australia Felix

After another four days, the party came to the spot where the Darling joined the Murray. They followed the Darling a little way upstream, but Mitchell was now convinced that it showed 'all the usual features of the Darling'. He decided to leave the banks of the Darling and follow the Murray in the opposite direction. On 21 June, he reached a lagoon near where the Loddon River joins the Murray and named it Swan Hill because of the abundance of 'swans and other wild fowl'. On 28 June, Mitchell climbed a hill which he called Mount Hope. Looking to the south-west, he saw country that he thought 'too inviting to be left behind us unexplored'. So, once again, he disobeyed Governor Bourke's orders and turned away from the Murray, moving through country that became more exciting the further he ventured into it. He celebrated the discovery of this lush and fertile section of western Victoria, where kangaroos and emus were abundant, by naming it 'Australia Felix' (Happy Australia).

In mid-July, in freezing weather, several of the party climbed a mountain range which Mitchell named the Grampians, after a range in his native Scotland. On 29 August, the party reached Portland Bay in south-western Victoria. Here Mitchell was surprised to find a ship at anchor and a number of wooden houses. At first he thought they belonged to bushrangers, but to his relief he found that they belonged to the Henty brothers who had come across from Tasmania to set up a secret farming enterprise. The Hentys entertained Mitchell most cordially and gave him much-needed supplies for the return journey.

Mitchell is remembered mainly for his discovery of the great agricultural lands of western Victoria, but his welcome home was not entirely happy. He was criticised by Bourke for his frequent clashes with Aborigines, and the bloody ambush at Mount Dispersion was subsequently investigated by the New South Wales parliament.

North again

Mitchell was extremely unlucky in his exploration of rivers. Despite his experience on the Barwon in 1831, he still held to his belief in a river that would provide a highway to the north, and in December 1845, he set out to search for it. In late July he began following the Belyando River in North Queensland, only to find that it petered out in swamps and channels. But in September he finally sighted the Barcoo. It was flowing to the north-west so strongly that Mitchell was convinced it would reach right to the Gulf of Carpentaria. He named it the Victoria and wrote that its discovery 'seemed like a reward from Heaven . . . for the many sacrifices I have made, in order to solve the question as to the interior rivers of Tropical Australia'. The following year another explorer was to prove Mitchell wrong and show that this river was an extension of Cooper Creek and flowed south-west into the interior of the continent.

The Henty brothers greet a surprised Mitchell as he arrives at Portland Bay.

ALPINE EXPLORERS

Australia's highest mountain, Mount Kosciuszko, the peak that rises just over 2200 metres in the Australian Alps, is named after a famous Polish patriot, Tadeusz Kosciuszko. It was named by the first European to climb it, Paul Edmund de Strzelecki. Strzelecki arrived in Sydney in 1839, at the age of 42, and the following year he led an expedition into the alpine region. Strzelecki was born and raised in Poland, but escaped to England in 1830 when he was accused of embezzling money. Although he was the son of poor parents he had an aristocratic charm and referred to himself as Count Strzelecki. With a strong interest in geology and mineralogy, Strzelecki explored widely in New South Wales, Victoria and Tasmania. But it was his mountain exploration that brought him fame.

Paul de Strzelecki

An alpine pioneer

Strzelecki's 1840 expedition was not the first one into the alps, nor was it the first one led by a Pole. In January 1834, almost ten years after Hume and Hovell first sighted the alps' snow-covered peaks, John Lhotsky, a Polish-born scientist who arrived in Australia in 1832, led a very ill-equipped party into these mountains. With four servants and a horse and cart he went south from Sydney in search of rocks and plant specimens. A month later the party was in the Southern Highlands and was soon in the alpine regions. We cannot be sure exactly where Lhotsky's journey took him, but on 6 March he climbed a mountain which he claimed, probably correctly, was the 'highest point ever [yet] reached by any traveller on the Australian continent'. From this point Lhotsky

could see the plains of the high country which lay further south around the present town of Omeo. This area is now covered by rich pastures. Lhotsky tried to reach these plains, but was prevented from doing so by the wide expanse of the Snowy River, which he was unable to cross.

Discovering Gippsland

The next two explorers in the region were Scotsmen looking for grazing land. In 1835, George Mackillop, who was squatting on land further north, found a way through to the Omeo plains by crossing the Snowy River further east than where Lhotsky had come upon it. In January 1840, Angus McMillan, manager of a station on the Monaro plains, went looking for grazing land for his employer, Lachlan McAlister. With a party of four white men and two Aborigines, McMillan pushed south and south-east from the Omeo plains through the rugged high country to discover the rich farming and grazing

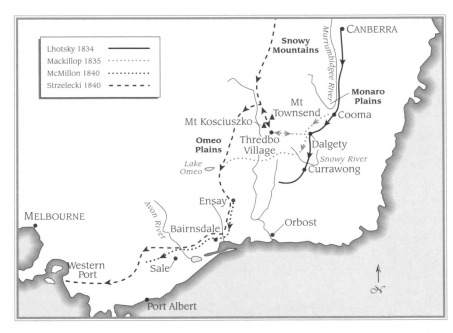

The routes of the alpine explorers.

Angus McMillan with two Aboriginal guides. In spite of the friendly appearance of this photograph, McMillan was responsible for the deaths of many Aborigines in the Gippsland area.

lands that are now known as Gippsland. According to McMillan, it was 'a country capable of supporting all my starving countrymen'. He named it 'Caledonia Australis'. The name 'Gipps Land' was given to this area by Strzelecki soon afterwards.

After climbing Mount Kosciuszko, Strzelecki proceeded further south and in March 1840, stopped at Ensay on the Omeo plains. Lachlan McAlister had established a station here that was run by his nephew Matthew McAlister. Matthew gave Strzelecki provisions and told him about McMillan's discoveries only two months before. Strzelecki then set off in the same direction and covered much of the same territory as McMillan, renaming the rivers as he went. Like McMillan,

Strzelecki was delighted with the rich country he found and he named it after the New South Wales governor, George Gipps. Except for Gippsland, all of McMillan's names were later restored.

Even though he knew of McMillan's expedition, Strzelecki later claimed that he was travelling through country 'hitherto untrodden by white man'. To be fair, Strzelecki's party did go further south than McMillan's. Thinking that the southern coast was closer than it actually was, they kept pushing south-west beyond the Avon River. With their provisions almost exhausted, they struggled through mountains, now known as the Strzelecki Range, to arrive on the eastern shores of Western Port on 12 May.

LUDWIG LEICHHARDT

Among the great explorers of Australia, only two disappeared without trace. The first was the maritime explorer George Bass, who disappeared at sea in 1803. The other was the German Ludwig Leichhardt. In 1848, with six men and a team of about 80 bullocks, Leichhardt set out from a point north of Brisbane in his second attempt to cross the Australian continent from east to west. In his first attempt, two years earlier, Leichhardt and the eight men who accompanied him had been forced to return to the coast, exhausted and suffering from tropical fevers after trekking for seven months. Although a total of nine major expeditions have gone in search of Leichhardt's party, his disappearance still remains perhaps the greatest mystery in Australian exploration.

Ludwig Leichhardt

When 28-year-old Leichhardt arrived in Sydney in February 1842, he knew nothing about bushcraft and suffered from poor eyesight. He had studied science and medicine in Berlin, where he and an English friend made plans to come to Australia. His friend changed his mind but generously paid Leichhardt's fare and gave him some extra money. Leichhardt had not graduated from university, but he nevertheless passed himself off as Doctor Leichhardt.

Leichhardt spent a good deal of time studying and collecting specimens of local plants and rocks, and became well known as an expert on botany. In 1843, he made a long and difficult solo journey on foot between Newcastle and Brisbane. Governor Gipps was planning an overland expedition to the settlement of Port Essington in Arnhem Land and Leichhardt may very well have been included in it. But when the expedition was delayed due to lack of funds, Leichhardt became impatient and decided to organise an expedition of his own. A number of business associates and some pastoralists, who were very interested in finding out what sort of country lay north of the Darling Downs, helped to finance the expedition.

The settlement at Port Essington in the 1840s.

The journey from Jimbour

On 1 October 1844, a party consisting of Leichhardt, seven Englishmen and two Aboriginal stockmen set out from Jimbour station on the Darling Downs. They had with them 17 horses, several bullocks and almost 1000 kilograms of food and other supplies. Leichhardt had decided not to strike directly across country, but to travel north up the eastern side of the Great Dividing Range where water was likely to be more plentiful. He then planned to turn west and keep close to the Gulf of Carpentaria. Within a month of leaving, the party experienced difficulties. A large amount of flour had been lost when the bags containing it were torn by thick bush, one of the bullocks had already been killed for food and two of the Englishmen had abandoned the party.

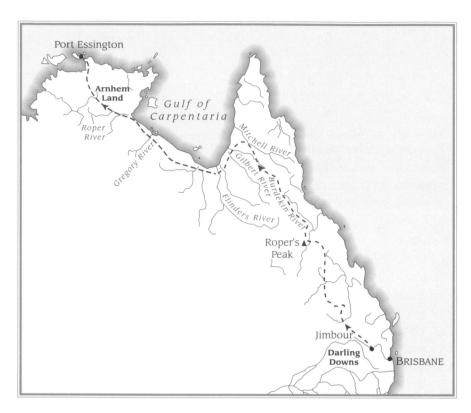

Leichhardt's 1844–45 expedition.

This picture, drawn by C.P. Hodgson, a member of Leichhardt's expedition, shows the party camped on the banks of the Dawson River in November 1844. Hodgson left the expedition and returned to Moreton Bay soon afterwards.

After five weeks of travelling, the party had covered only about 150 kilometres. Leichhardt did not seem to be in a hurry and the men took time to collect and examine plants, particularly as they moved further north into the exotic tropical regions. It was not long before their provisions began to run low and many of their meals consisted of stews made from cockatoos, emus, kangaroos, goannas, fish, eels or any other animal they managed to catch.

A fatal attack

Almost nine months after setting out, the party was near the eastern edge of the Gulf of Carpentaria when the first real tragedy struck. On 28 June 1845, the party was camped on the edge of a lagoon when, at about 7 o'clock in the evening, a shower of spears rained down on the unsuspecting explorers. After replying with a round of gunfire, Leichhardt discovered that John Gilbert, the expedition's naturalist and most experienced bushman, had been speared through the neck and was dead. Two other men were seriously wounded. Three days later the expedition continued its westward journey with the two wounded men draped across the backs of horses. On 12 July, the party crossed a small river that flowed towards the Gulf of Carpentaria. Leichhardt named it the Gilbert in memory of his dead friend.

Trees marked by Leichhardt were found after his disappearance.

As they travelled across the plains near the Gulf of Carpentaria, they were able to make faster progress. The country was more open, there was no shortage of water and wildlife for food was plentiful. On 19 October, they reached a large river which Leichhardt named after John Roper, the first member of the group to spot it. Here they encountered another setback when three of their horses slid down the river's steep banks and drowned.

The last two months of the journey were particularly difficult. By this stage their clothes were hanging off them in strips and they had eaten the last of their bullocks. The rest of their journey lay across the rocky ridges of the Arnhem Tableland. Their lives were probably saved by groups of friendly Aborigines who helped them find food and guided them on their way. Just 15 days before they stumbled into Port Essington on 17 December 1845, they were heartened when an Aborigine whom they met asked them in English, 'What's your name?' They knew then that they were close to their destination.

At the end of March 1846, the survivors of this epic journey arrived back in Sydney where they were given a rapturous welcome. People had long since given them up for dead.

EDMUND KENNEDY

When Thomas Mitchell chose his party for his 1845 expedition to the north, he selected a 27-year-old surveyor, Edmund Kennedy, as his second-in-command. Kennedy had arrived in Australia in 1840 at the age of 21, and was experienced in leading survey parties around the difficult country in the Port Phillip district. In 1847, Mitchell was about to leave for London to oversee the publication of his account of his northern journey. He was keen to have proof that the river he had named the Victoria flowed northward right to the Gulf of Carpentaria. So, he appointed Kennedy to lead an expedition for that purpose.

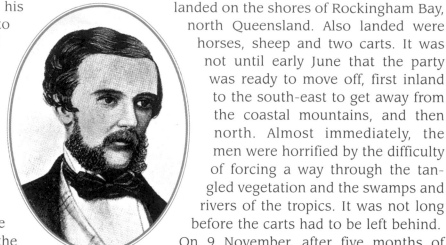

Edmund Kennedy

The journey was long and difficult. It lasted nine months and almost ended in tragedy when the party's provisions were destroyed by Aborigines. Unfortunately for Mitchell and his reputation, Kennedy found that the Victoria, which he renamed the Barcoo, did not continue to the north but turned south-west to become part of Cooper Creek.

The mystery of Cape York

But what was the far north-east of the continent really like? Sir Charles Fitzroy, who was now the governor of New South Wales, wanted to find out. In 1848, he appointed Kennedy to take a party up the east coast of Cape York, down the western coast and then further south to link up with the area that he had previously explored. A ship would be sent to meet the party near the tip of Cape York and to replenish their provisions.

Despite the careful planning, this turned out to be one of the most disastrous of all journeys of exploration; of the 13 men who set out, only three survived. On 21 May 1848, after a 22-day voyage from Sydney, the party was

landed on the shores of Rockingham Bay, north Queensland. Also landed were horses, sheep and two carts. It was not until early June that the party was ready to move off, first inland to the south-east to get away from the coastal mountains, and then north. Almost immediately, the men were horrified by the difficulty of forcing a way through the tangled vegetation and the swamps and rivers of the tropics. It was not long before the carts had to be left behind.

On 9 November, after five months of arduous trekking, the party reached Weymouth Bay about 700 kilometres north of their starting point. By this time eight men were too ill to continue and Kennedy left them there with some provisions and two horses. Only two days later, one of the remaining five men was seriously wounded when he accidentally shot himself in the shoulder. Kennedy left him and two others at Shelburne Bay and continued with only one companion, an Aboriginal guide called Jackey Jackey. They were heading for Port Albany at the tip of Cape York where a ship was to meet them. But the two men were in a very weak condition and were being pursued by a group of hostile Aborigines.

Kennedy's death

About a month after leaving Shelburne Bay, in the swampy estuary of the Escape River barely 50 kilometres south of Port Albany, the men found that they were surrounded. Kennedy was speared in several places and Jackey Jackey was wounded above the eye. Jackey Jackey managed to shoot one of the attackers, but they returned and speared Kennedy again in the leg. Kennedy died soon afterwards and Jackey Jackey was able to escape along a creek, keeping only his head above water. He arrived at Port Albany

The route of Kennedy's fatal journey.

Kennedy is speared to death.

on 23 December to relate to Captain Dobson, whose ship, the *Ariel*, had been waiting there for two months, the sorry story of their journey. Dobson sailed down the coast to rescue the men who had been left behind. There was no trace of the three men left at Shelburne Bay, and of the eight at Weymouth Bay, only two were still alive. One of them, William Carron, the expedition's botanist, was almost unconscious and had to be carried on board.

EDWARD JOHN EYRE

The Eyre Highway runs across the Nullarbor Plain. For much of its length it skirts the very southern shores of the continent and roughly follows the route taken by the first expedition to cross this harsh, almost waterless expanse. This expedition took eight months to complete, from late 1840 until July 1841, and the leader was 26-year-old Englishman Edward John Eyre.

Eyre had at first seemed destined for an army career, but his father persuaded him to come to Australia because of his delicate health. He arrived in 1833, at the age of 17. For some time he was a farmer, but in 1837 Eyre met Charles Sturt in Sydney, and Sturt encouraged him to drove cattle overland to Port Phillip. Eyre did this, then drove both sheep and cattle overland from Port Phillip to Adelaide in the recently established colony of South Australia. Early in 1840, he sailed across the Great Australian Bight and then drove cattle from Albany to Perth. But before this, the enterprising young Eyre had already done some exploring.

Edward John Eyre

The search for grazing land

In 1839, the settlement at Adelaide was only three years old and the settlers there had very little idea of what sort of country lay to the north. In May 1839, Eyre, accompanied by three Europeans and two Aborigines, set out from Adelaide and headed north, hoping to find rich grazing country. For some time they travelled through the rich country between the Gawler and Hutt rivers, but after that the country soon turned barren and sandy. The party came in sight of the rugged time-worn Flinders Ranges and a vast salt lake to the west, which Eyre named Lake Torrens. In August 1839, Eyre set out again, this time from Port Lincoln on the south-western edge of Spencer Gulf, to explore the area that is now known as the Eyre Peninsula. Once again, he was discouraged to find only dry, arid country.

Many people in South Australia were keen to know what lay to the west. Perhaps grazing lands could be found there and a stock route opened up to Western Australia. Eyre, however, suggested that an expedition to the north would be more useful and, with Sturt's support, he persuaded the authorities to sponsor one. On 18 June 1840, a party of eight men was given a rousing send-off after break-fasting at Government House. With their group of 13 horses and 40 sheep, they were to travel as far north as possible — right to the centre of the continent, or even as far as the north coast! On 8 July, the expedition came to Lake Torrens but its salt-encrusted, boggy surface was absolutely impossible to cross.

Eyre then decided to follow the Flinders Ranges. He hoped to find water and grass in their gorges and also hoped that these ranges would extend right into the interior. But his hopes were dashed when he climbed a mountain, only to see the way forward barred by what looked like a ring of salt lakes. The biggest of them, which Eyre thought was still part of Lake Torrens, was in fact the southern section of Lake Eyre. The disappointed party returned, not to Adelaide, but to Port Lincoln. From here, Eyre sent reports to the governor and began to plan a continuation of his expedition, this time not to the north, but westward across the Nullarbor Plain.

Westward at last

On 17 November, Eyre arrived at Fowlers Bay, a whaling station about 800 kilometres north-west of Port Lincoln. It was the last port of call along the Great Australian Bight and was therefore the last place to which supplies could be delivered. The governor of South Australia, Sir George Gawler, was not happy with Eyre's change of plan and wrote to tell him so. But Eyre was determined, despite the dangers.

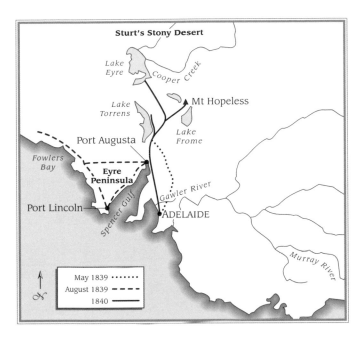

Eyre's expeditions, 1839–40

In the next three months the party made three attempts to move westward, but was driven back each time by heat and lack of water. Already three horses had died. In order to travel more lightly, Eyre decided to take only four men with him: his second-in-command, John Baxter, and three Aboriginal guides. He sent the others back to Adelaide. On 25 February 1841, the four men set out with 11 horses and six sheep, bound for Albany at the far end of the Bight.

Throughout the gruelling journey water was almost always in short supply, and only the lucky find of Aboriginal wells underneath sandhills saved them. A number of times the men were forced to kill their horses for food, and the fly-blown meat caused them to suffer from attacks of dysentery. On 29 April, just over two months into their journey, the party was camped near a place now called Twilight Cove, when Eyre was startled by a gunshot nearby. Wylie, one of the Aboriginal guides, called to him in alarm and Eyre ran to find Baxter bleeding and close to death. The two other Aborigines, desperate for food, had shot Baxter and had run off with the last two good rifles and some of the remaining food.

Baxter was an old and trusted friend and his loss filled Eyre with horror and foreboding. Leaving Baxter's body wrapped in a sheet — the ground was too hard to dig — Eyre and Wylie pressed on. Three weeks later, they were close to death but were saved by a change in the landscape. At a point on the coast near the Russell Ranges, they found a spot where sand and scrub gave way to grass and where there was something they had not seen since they started out — running water. They were also able catch kangaroos and fish. They stayed here for seven days, then continued on, even though they were still ill and weak.

A change of fortune

It is unlikely that they would have completed their journey without one final and seemingly miraculous stroke of fortune. On 2 June, as they rounded a bend in the coast, they saw the masts of a ship. Eyre made a fire to attract attention and soon after, a boat set out for shore to pick them up.

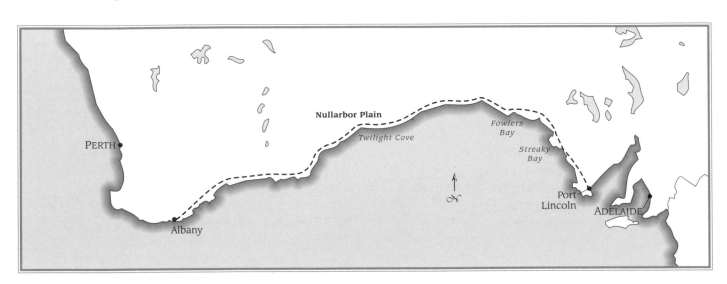

Eyre's journey to the west, 1840–41

Eyre and Wylie near the end of their journey across the Nullarbor.

They had happened upon the French whaling vessel *Mississippi*, which was commanded by an Englishman, Captain Rossiter. Rossiter took them in, fed them for 12 days and gave them new clothes. Eyre named the bay where they met their rescuers Rossiter Bay.

On 15 June, they resumed their journey. As if to compensate for the earlier lack of water, heavy rain fell almost constantly during the last weeks of their trek. The night of 6 June, the last before they arrived in Albany, Eyre described as yet 'another night's misery . . . for we had hardly lain down before the rain began to fall again in torrents'.

People in Albany and Adelaide had thought them long dead, and as they were seen descending into the town, they were mobbed by an excited crowd. Six days after arriving, they sailed for Adelaide where they were treated to a grand official dinner. Charles Sturt, Eyre's admiring friend and mentor, was among the guests.

Eyre and Wylie's achievement lay more in the heroism they displayed than in any real benefits their expedition brought. It did not open up new pasture or agricultural lands or stock routes. Rather, it confirmed that between Adelaide and Perth there lay a huge, arid and forbidding wilderness.

JOHN McDOUALL STUART

In 1862, when Charles Sturt heard the news that John McDouall Stuart had succeeded in crossing the continent from south to north, his reaction was to comment, 'I always knew him to be a plucky little fellow'. Plucky he certainly was, and little too — but Stuart was also fiercely determined, perhaps more so than any other Australian explorer. When Stuart finally achieved his goal, it was on his third attempt. Three times he had defied the hazards of heat, thirst, hunger and disease, as well as the dangers of attack, to venture into the heart of the continent. As he set out on his final expedition in

Chambers Pillar

January 1862, even the knowledge that he could no longer be the first to make the south-to-north crossing did not detract from his enthusiasm for the task.

By 1860 Stuart was an experienced explorer, and at the age of 44 he was no longer a young man. He had arrived in Australia in 1839 and had first worked as a surveyor. In 1844, he was part of the expedition Charles Sturt led into the desert in the fruitless search for an inland sea. In the late 1850s, Stuart led several expeditions to the north of Adelaide, especially around Lake Eyre, discovering and naming numerous water-courses and mountains. On at least one of these expeditions, he almost died of starvation. So, when he responded in 1860 to the South Australian government's offer of 2000 pounds to the first person to lead an expedition right across the continent from south to north, he had no illusions about the rigours ahead.

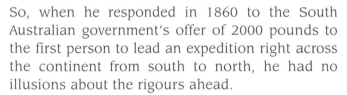

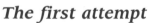

John McDouall Stuart

By now the party was in the arid, sandy country that is typical of central Australia and was in fact approaching the very centre of the continent. They reached what Stuart calculated by observing the sun to be the centre on the evening of 21 April. The next day, Stuart and his second-in-command, Kekwick, climbed a nearby hill. There they built up a mound of stones and planted in it a pole bearing the British flag. Stuart named the hill Central Mount Sturt, in honour of his famous friend, however, it has always been known since as Central Mount Stuart.

By early May the strain of the journey was beginning to tell. Provisions were running low, water was scarce and hard to find, and Stuart was experiencing the first signs of scurvy. On 13 May, Stuart fell from his horse and injured himself,

The first attempt

On 2 March 1860, Stuart set out from Chambers Creek, just south of Lake Eyre, with two other men and 13 horses. The party experienced problems right from the start. Only a few days into their journey, they were slowed down by heavy rain and one of the horses drowned as they crossed a flooded creek. A few weeks later, on 1 April, Stuart became aware that his right eye was severely damaged from the strain of taking observations from the sun over many years. On 4 April, while passing through what Stuart described as 'splendid country', they arrived at a stream surrounded by tall gums. Stuart named it the Finke after William Finke, who had provided money for some of his earlier expeditions. Two days later, Stuart came upon a tall, spectacular sandstone formation rising like a tower from the plain. He named this Chambers Pillar after William Chambers, who had helped finance this and earlier expeditions. Nearby, there was a rugged, rocky mountain range. Stuart named it the MacDonnell Range, after the governor of South Australia.

and the party retreated to Central Mount Stuart to rest. However, they ventured on again until 26 June, when they came to a creek just a little north of the present town of Tennant Creek. Here a group of hostile Aborigines burnt the grass around the explorers' camp and attacked them with boomerangs. Fearing further attacks and realising that he and his companions were too weak to continue, Stuart reluctantly decided to turn back. The place they reached was appropriately named Attack Creek. On the return journey they were fortunate to discover crops of native vegetables which relieved the effects of scurvy.

A rival expedition

When Stuart returned to Adelaide in October, he learnt that another expedition bound for the north, led by Robert O'Hara Burke, had set out from Melbourne just two months earlier. This spurred Stuart on to make another attempt and this time he had the backing of the South Australian government, which did not want Victoria to claim the honour. The South Australian government contributed 2500 pounds to the expedition and this enabled Stuart to take a larger, better-equipped team of 12 men and 49 horses.

McDouall Stuart and Kekwick raise the British flag on Central Mount Stuart, near the centre of the continent.

The expedition left Chambers Creek in January 1861, following the route of the previous one. It made good time: by mid-March it had reached the Finke River and by April it had passed the point where the previous expedition was abandoned. Stuart set up a base camp about 50 kilometres north of Attack Creek on the banks of a stream which he generously named Burke Creek, after his rival. Unknown to him, Burke had already won the race to the north coast, but was now struggling to survive the return journey. From Burke Creek, Stuart tried several times to force a way through to the north. But beyond a place he called Newcastle Waters, he was unable to get across a vast, seemingly waterless plain. On returning to Burke Creek,

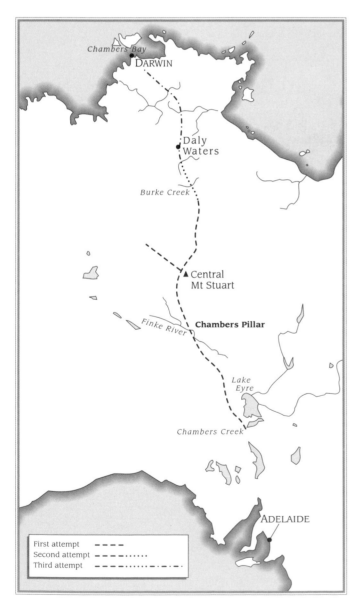

In 1862 Stuart succeeded in his south–north crossing.

Stuart found that Aborigines had attacked the camp and chased away the horses. On 12 July, with his men in rags and with his provisions running out, he again turned back in defeat.

Determination rewarded

Stuart arrived back in Adelaide in late September. Although Burke and several other members of his expedition were by this time dead, there was still no news of that expedition's fate. Stuart immediately set about planning a third attempt. He managed to convince the government to help finance a new expedition and in January 1862, he set out again, leading 10 men and 71 horses.

By early April Stuart was back at Newcastle Waters and was moving further north into new territory. On 10 May he entered a dense mulga forest. Rather than try to go through it, he headed north-east. On 23 May, he came upon a creek which led him into rich, wooded and well-grassed country. He named the area Daly Waters. At this stage he noted in his journal that he was now even more weary than he had been the previous year and that he could feel his 'capability of endurance beginning to give way'. He went on, however, following a number of streams, and naming the Katherine and Mary rivers. On 24 July, the party broke through dense bushes to find themselves on a beach on the northern coast. A delighted Stuart named the place Chambers Bay.

After this superb achievement, Stuart was lucky to survive the return journey. By late August the party was almost back at Daly Waters, but Stuart was again in the grip of scurvy and could hardly eat. By late October he wrote that he was 'in the grasp of death'; he was almost blind and could no longer walk. He hung on, however, and by 10 December, he had reached a friend's property about 500 kilometres north of Adelaide. He rested and recovered there, and on 21 January 1863 he and his party rode into Adelaide where they were given a hero's welcome.

Stuart was not the first to cross the continent, but the route that he blazed was followed soon afterwards by the Overland Telegraph Line. This established communications between Adelaide and Darwin and linked Australia with the rest of the world. Stuart's health never recovered fully from the damage his last expedition had inflicted and he died less than four years later.

BURKE AND WILLS

In all of John McDouall Stuart's expeditions, not a single human life was lost. Stuart was a courageous explorer who was willing to take risks, but he had the good sense to know when the risks were too great and had the prudence to give up when he knew there was no chance of success. But the expedition led by Robert O'Hara Burke, which left Melbourne on 20 August 1860 to the cheers of 15 000 people and a rousing speech from the mayor of Melbourne, was a very different story. Of the 18 men who set out, six did not return and of the four men who actually reached the northern shores of the continent, only one survived. The story of Robert O'Hara Burke's expedition is one of poor leadership and foolhardy decisions, as well as sheer bad luck.

Melbourne was a booming city in 1860. The Victorian gold rushes of the 1850s had brought great prosperity and a feeling that anything was achievable. Stuart's first attempt to cross the continent had received a lot of publicity and a Melbourne organisation called the Royal Society decided that Victoria should have the honour of sponsoring the first successful crossing. It raised 9000 pounds to finance the expedition and sent an Englishman, George Landells, to India to bring back 25 camels for it. The expedition set out, taking with it a total of 27 camels and 23 horses. Landells was second-in-command.

Burke was perhaps a strange choice for leader. He arrived in Melbourne from his native Ireland in 1853, at the age of 32. He had been a mounted police-man in Ireland,

Robert O'Hara Burke

William John Wills

and he joined the Victorian police immediately. He had no experience as an explorer and very little experience of the bush. In 1857 he had managed to get lost in the bush when he had gone out to quell a riot on one of the goldfields. Otherwise, however, his police record was a good one. An actress with whom Burke was in love had supposedly promised to marry him if he was successful in reaching the northern coast.

The third in charge of this ill-fated expedition was 26-year-old William John Wills. He had studied medicine for a short time before he came to Victoria in 1853 and began work as a surveyor. Before joining this expedition, Wills had never been into the desert.

This cartoon, representing the 'race' between Burke's and Stuart's expeditions, appeared in the **Melbourne Punch**
on 8 November 1860.

To the Victorian public, Burke's expedition had all the excitement and drama of a great sporting event. A Melbourne newspaper published some verses, depicting it as a 'race . . . from south to northern shore!' and comparing Stuart and Burke, and their different means of transport, in the following terms:

The horseman hails from Adelaide
The camel rider's ours:—
Now let the steed maintain his speed,
Against the camel's powers.

Early troubles

It took the expedition almost two months to reach the settlement of Menindee on the Darling, but even before that there was trouble. Landells had brought along large amounts of rum to feed to the camels and their drivers, presumably to protect them from scurvy. When Burke questioned this practice, the two men quarrelled and Landells left the expedition, taking several others with him. Wills then became second-in-command.

At Menindee, Burke decided to split up the party. He went north with seven men and 15 camels to set up a base camp on Cooper Creek, as he had been instructed. He arrived there in October. Cooper Creek was not flowing, but they were able to obtain water from a number of large waterholes in the area. Burke sent one of the men, William Wright, back to Menindee to collect the rest of the party and the provisions. By mid-December the others had not turned up and Burke's impatience got the better of him. He split the party once again. Despite the advice that another distinguished explorer, Augustus Gregory, had given him not to go into the desert in the heat of summer, Burke decided to set out. He left on 16 December, taking with him Wills and two other men, Charles Gray and John King. On this final 1100-kilometre dash to the northern coast, they took six camels and one horse.

Left behind at Cooper Creek

William Brahe was left in charge of the camp on Cooper Creek, which was christened Fort Wills. Brahe had instructions to wait at Fort Wills for three months and then, if Burke's group did not return, to go back to Melbourne. Brahe and the others at Fort Wills waited more than four months until, ill with scurvy, they decided to head south on the morning of 21 April 1861. If they had waited only a few more hours, three tragic deaths would probably have been avoided.

Eight days later, Brahe's group met Wright with the group from Menindee and they had a sorry story to tell. Within a month of leaving Menindee, two men had died of scurvy and the very day before the meeting with Brahe, the expedition's artist, Ludwig Becker, had also succumbed to the disease. Although he had decided to go no further, Wright agreed to go with Brahe back to Fort Wills, just in case the others had turned up. When they got there they found no sign of Burke's team, so they left again.

Towards the northern coast

When they left Fort Wills, Burke's team made good progress. Once they had crossed Sturt's Stony Desert, the harsh gibber plain that Sturt had discovered, they were in country that no European had ever seen before. As they pushed northward, the dry country gave way to tropical swamps and marshes and the camels found the going very difficult. When they were quite close to their destination, and with supplies running low, Burke split the team for the last time. With Wills and one horse, Burke covered the last 50 kilometres to arrive, on 11 February, at the mangrove swamps that bordered the sea near the mouth of the Flinders River. They could not see the sea, but they knew they had reached their goal.

Burke and Wills returned to Gray and King and the party began its homeward journey. Their provisions were almost exhausted and they had to find food along the way. On one occasion they killed and ate a large snake, which made Burke violently ill. More serious though, was the steadily weakening condition of Gray. On 25 March, Burke found him stealing flour and gave him a severe beating. Almost a month later, on 17 April, Gray, who was now being carried draped across the back of a camel, died.

Four days after Gray's death, the other three reached Fort Wills. There they found a message burnt into the trunk of a coolibah tree: 'Dig 3 ft N.W. Apr. 21 1861'. Brahe and his team had left only a few hours earlier. The provisions they dug up saved their lives — at least for the moment.

A fateful decision

Burke then decided, against Wills' and King's wishes, not to follow Brahe, but to head south-west. He hoped to reach Mount Hopeless in South Australia, where he knew there was a police outpost. They set off from Fort Wills on 23 April, leaving a note buried in the sand. But they did not leave a sign to indicate where the note was. When Brahe and Wright returned to Fort Wills soon afterwards, they did not find this note.

As Burke, Wills and King made their way along Cooper Creek a band of Aborigines helped them to find food. However, when Burke surprised one of the Aborigines trying to steal something from the provisions, he impetuously fired his gun in the

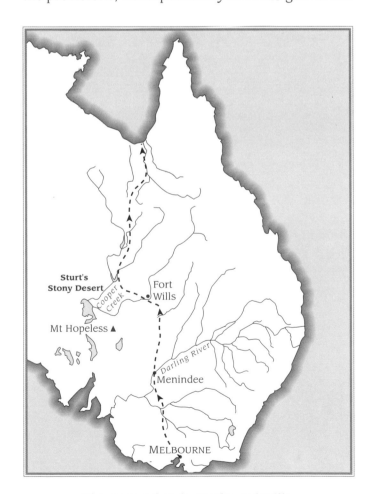

The route taken by Burke and Wills.

air and frightened their saviours away. This was the beginning of the end for the three explorers. From this point onwards they began starving to death. Towards the end of June, Wills died. Burke survived him by only two days.

Almost three months later, on 21 September, a rescue party that had set out from Melbourne found King living in the desert, being cared for by a group of Aborigines. Burke's and Wills' remains were found and buried near Cooper Creek. Later they were dug up and brought back to Melbourne, where the two explorers were given a huge public funeral.

The funeral of Burke and Wills in Melbourne.

King guides his rescuers to the remains of Burke and Wills.

ERNEST GILES

By the 1860s most of the burning questions about the interior of Australia had been answered. Stuart's journeys had shown the nature of the centre, and the notion of an inland sea had long been laid to rest. But there were still important mysteries to be solved about vast areas of the west. An explorer who solved many of these was Ernest Giles.

Giles arrived in Adelaide from England in 1850, at the age of 15. For some time he tried his luck on the Victorian goldfields, but without much success. He then tried his hand at a number of occupations until he ended up, in 1861, in the area around Menindee in western New South Wales. In 1865, with his old school friend William Tietkins, he explored to the west of the Darling River, in search of land that would be suitable for pastoral use.

Ernest Giles

A convenient starting place

In 1872, the Overland Telegraph Line between Adelaide and Darwin was completed and stations built along this line provided convenient starting places for expeditions to the west. In the same year Ferdinand von Mueller, the Victorian government botanist and a friend of Giles, asked Giles to lead a small expedition from the Charlotte Waters station, near Chambers Pillar, in an attempt to go overland to Perth. This party set out in August, following the Finke River and discovering the wonderful enclosed valley of palms that is now called Palm Valley. Further on, however, the party was forced back when it encountered harsh deserts and a vast salt lake that von Mueller insisted be named Lake Amadeus, after the king of Spain.

The next year, in August 1873, von Mueller sent Giles on another expedition, this time with Tietkins as second-in-charge. It began at Alberga Creek and was once again bound for Perth. This time Giles went further south to avoid Lake Amadeus, but once again harsh desert conditions defeated him. A young stockman, Alf Gibson, who had volunteered to go on the expedition, was lost in the desert and never found. Giles named the desert in which he disappeared the Gibson Desert.

Travelling with camels

In May 1875, Giles' most important expedition began from Beltana, north of Port Augusta. It was financed mainly by Thomas Elder, a prominent Adelaide businessman and pastoralist. This time, instead of horses, Giles took 22 camels and an Afghan camel driver called Sahleh, who had accompanied the explorer Peter Warburton in his epic 1873 expedition across the northern part of Western Australia. Once again Tietkins was second-in-charge and four others, including an Aboriginal guide, completed the party.

Over the next six months, the party trekked over the vast waterless wastes of the Great Victoria Desert, which Giles named after the British queen. The camels certainly proved their worth on this expedition; at one stage they travelled 350 kilometres without being able to drink. Several times the party had to change direction or retrace its steps when supplies of water ran low and none could be found. As they set out deeper into the unknown, Giles offered his men the chance to turn back, taking camels and food with them. But not one of them took up the offer. Late in September, with all the water they were carrying finished, they were saved only by the skill of their Aboriginal guide, who managed to follow emu tracks to a spring. In mid-October, at a point to the north-west of the present-day town of Kalgoorlie, they were attacked by a large band of Aborigines who dispersed only after the explorers fired at them.

Giles' party arrives in Perth.

Early in November, the party came upon the most outlying of the West Australian sheep stations. Now they were safe and were able to turn south-west for Perth, passing through a series of settlements. The news of their successful crossing soon spread and they entered Perth to a rousing reception by the mayor, other local dignitaries and a huge crowd of citizens.

Returning the hard way

After such a long and gruelling expedition, Giles might have been expected to rest. But, as he later wrote, 'I regarded what had been done as only half of my mission'. He was determined to make another crossing, this time starting from the west and crossing the Gibson Desert.

To Giles' annoyance, Tietkins and one other member of the party refused to make the return journey and went back to South Australia by ship. On 13 January 1876, Giles, Sahleh and two others took their camel team north from Perth to the area near Geraldton, then north-west to the Ashburton River. They camped here for 13 days before setting off into the Gibson Desert. For the next three-and-a-half weeks, the party made its way across 'ceaseless undulations of sand' in a region that, according to Giles, was 'so desolate that it is horrifying even to describe'. By the end of

June, Giles was back in the desert he had first reached in 1874. He searched once more, without success, for Alf Gibson's remains. He then continued eastwards to arrive at the Overland Telegraph Line near the end of August.

Giles described his own journeys of exploration in a book that was published in 1889 and which was titled *Australia Twice Traversed*. In this book Giles made the following modest assessment of his considerable achievements: 'though I shall not attempt to rank myself amongst the first or greatest, yet I think I have reason to call myself, the last of the Australian explorers'.

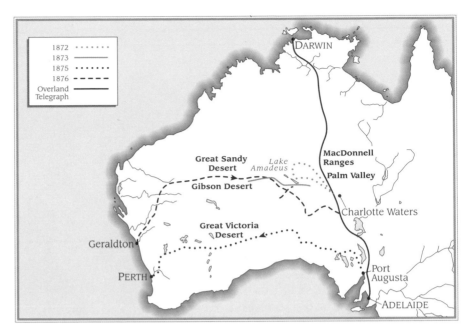

Giles' expeditions shed further light on the nature of the land to the west.

Giles' own sketch of Palm Valley on the Finke River. Giles called it the Glen of Palms.

WARBURTON AND GOSSE

In 1873, 13 years after the famous race to the north of the continent between John McDouall Stuart and Robert O'Hara Burke, two determined explorers once again lined up for a race. This time, however, both expeditions were heading west and they were both leaving from the same place. One of them was led by William Gosse, a 30-year-old surveyor who had little exploring experience, but who had been appointed by the South Australian government to find a route from Alice Springs to Perth. The other was under the command of Peter Warburton, who was almost 60 years old. Warburton, a former major in the British army in India, had arrived in Adelaide in 1853 to become the commissioner of police. However, in 1867, he lost his job when he fell out with the colonial authorities. Warburton had already led a number of excursions into the interior of South Australia and had explored the area around Lake Eyre. He was annoyed that Gosse had been chosen ahead of him to lead the official expedition. With the help of Thomas Elder, who supplied camels from his stud at Beltana in South Australia, and another businessman, Captain Walter Hughes, Warburton organised his own expedition. Thomas Elder also supplied camels for Gosse's expedition.

Warburton led a party of seven that included his son Richard, an Aboriginal guide and two Afghan camel drivers. One of the camel drivers, Sahleh, was later to accompany Ernest Giles in his 1875 crossing of the continent. The party took 17 camels but no horses and left Alice Springs on 15 April 1873. Just over a week

Peter Warburton

William Gosse

later, on 23 April, Gosse's expedition also set out from Alice Springs. As well as Gosse, it consisted of four Europeans, three Afghan camel drivers and an Aboriginal guide.

Across the Great Sandy Desert

Of the two leaders, Warburton proved the more resolute and determined. His expedition succeeded in reaching the west coast, though its overland journey took it not to Perth, but to a cattle station on the De Grey River in the north-west. It was a gruelling and torturous journey. After travelling for eight-and-a-half months across the wastes of the Great Sandy Desert, they finally reached their destination, but all the camels were dead. A number of them had died from weakness and thirst, several had succumbed to the fatal effects of poisonous plants and the rest had been killed and eaten to keep the humans in the group alive. The men were shrivelled wrecks, all suffering from scurvy, and Warburton had lost his sight in one eye.

During June and July, Sahleh almost died from scurvy. He was saved only by the discovery of a nutritious yellow berry which proved, fortunately, not to be poisonous. In the desperate search for water, Warburton resorted several times to capturing and mistreating Aborigines to force them to reveal the location of water-holes in the area.

Despite his ordeal, Warburton recovered his health and lived for another 16 years. He had the honour to be the first explorer to cross the western half of the continent, a clear winner in the race against Gosse.

Warburton's expedition sets out from Alice Springs in 1873. Warburton is the bearded figure at the front.

Defeated by the desert

Gosse's journey lasted almost as long as Warburton's, but desert conditions and lack of water frustrated his attempts to push far to the west. In December he ended up back at the Overland Telegraph Line at a point about 300 kilometres south of Alice Springs. The achievement for which he is now remembered is his discovery of Australia's best known natural landmark. On 19 July 1873, he was astonished to find 'one immense rock rising abruptly from the plain'. He named it Ayers Rock after a premier of South Australia and became the first of many millions of Europeans to climb to the top of it. Ayers Rock is now more commonly known by its traditional Aboriginal name, Uluru.

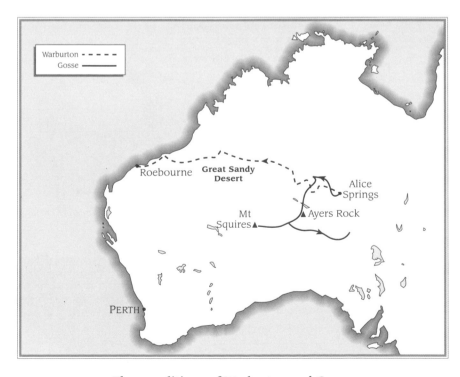

The expeditions of Warburton and Gosse.

JOHN AND ALEXANDER FORREST

When Ernest Giles' party made its triumphant entry into Perth after crossing from the Overland Telegraph Line in 1875, John Forrest was prominent among the welcoming dignitaries. Forrest was a strong supporter of Giles and was himself a famous explorer. He had already led an expedition across the western half of the continent, but in the opposite direction to Giles. Born and bred in Western Australia, Forrest was destined to make a name for himself, first as an explorer, then as the first premier of the colony of Western Australia and, after Federation in 1901, as a prominent member of several Australian governments.

Forrest had been a surveyor for four years when, in 1869 at the age of 22, he was sent out from Perth to the north-east to investigate reports that Aborigines had discovered the remains of the long lost explorer Ludwig Leichhardt. All the expedition discovered, however, were some horse's bones.

John Forrest

Crossing from west to east

The next year the governor of Western Australia, Sir Frederick Weld, sent Forrest on a much longer expedition — this time the intention was to traverse the south-west of the continent in search of the grazing land that Edward John Eyre had failed to discover during his expedition almost 30 years earlier. The party of six men, which included Forrest's younger brother, Alexander, virtually followed Eyre's route in reverse. Forrest, however, made frequent diversions to the north where he found a good deal of grassy country, but very few signs of water. The expedition was carefully planned and at two points along the way the men were

Alexander Forrest

met by a ship carrying supplies. At the end of August, five months after leaving Perth, the party arrived in Adelaide. The horses were much the worse for wear, but the men were in reasonable condition. They were warmly welcomed by a waiting crowd and were given an official reception at Government House.

Forrest's next expedition, in 1874, again had Alexander Forrest as second-in-charge, and again involved a crossing from west to east. This time it followed a much more northerly route. Setting out from Perth in March, the party of 6 men and 21 horses — unlike some other desert explorers, Forrest did not use camels — travelled north to the settlement of Geraldton and then north-east to the Murchison River. As they followed the Murchison to its source, they passed through splendid grassy country. At the beginning of June, they arrived at a spot where Forrest noted there was an 'almost unlimited . . . supply of water and feed'. Forrest named the place Weld Springs, after the governor of Western Australia. It was the most northerly point the expedition reached.

From here they turned south-east, then east through a great dry plain which Forrest described as 'an awful, desolate spinifex desert'. From this point on, the journey was a constant struggle. They moved slowly from one meagre water source to another until, just over the border with South Australia, they came upon another good spring. Forrest named this after Thomas Elder. The six-month trek across the interior finished at the end of August when the party reached the Overland Telegraph Line a little north of Peake Telegraph Station.

John Forrest's 1874 expedition in the spinifex desert.

The crossing was a magnificent achievement but Forrest's assessment of it was a rather sombre one. Very little pasture land had been found and all of it was quite close to the coast. Of the grassy patches found further inland, Forrest commented that 'they are so isolated, and of such extent, that it would never pay to stock them'.

A few years later, however, Alexander Forrest was responsible for opening up significant areas of sheep and cattle country. In 1879, he led an expedition of eight men from Roeborne, in the far north-west, up the coast to Beagle Bay, then inland into the area now known as the Kimberleys. They discovered rich country around the Fitzroy River, but when they went north they found their way blocked by the King Leopold Range. Returning south, they again followed the Fitzroy and found more fine grazing land. Further east they discovered a river that Forrest named the Ord, after the then governor of Western Australia. Shortage of food forced them to keep moving and they were unable to explore this river more closely. The rest of the journey to the Overland Telegraph Line was through arid, waterless country. Sheep and cattle soon followed Forrest's route into the north-west.

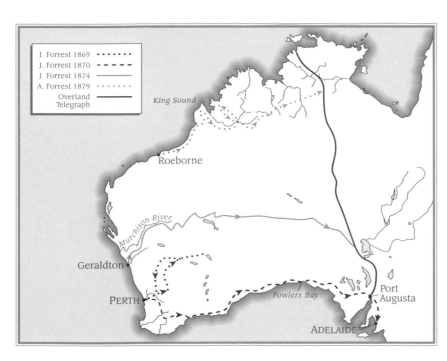

J. Forrest 1869 ·······
J. Forrest 1870 -------
J. Forrest 1874 ———
A. Forrest 1879 ·······
Overland Telegraph ———

King Sound

Roeborne

Murchison River

Geraldton

PERTH

Fowlers Bay

Port Augusta

ADELAIDE

The expeditions of the Forrest brothers.

INDEX